Pra

Grandparenting

"Eda LeShan has done it again. She has conspired to bring grand-parents out of the shadows and back into the world of children where they belong. She courageously reveals her deepest thoughts and emotions openly and honestly. Mrs. LeShan's wisdom and wit are presented lovingly to the grateful reader."

—Dr. Lawrence Balter,
psychologist and author

"This lovely book, so full of humanity and wisdom, is an invaluable guide to grandparenting."

—Judith Viorst

"In a world marked by social upheavals and a transformation of the traditional family structure . . . sound advice on grandparenting from psychologist, columnist, and grandmother LeShan . . . Common sense presented with uncommon grace."

—*Kirkus Reviews*

"This open-minded, open-hearted, and insightful book explores what is different and what is timeless about contemporary grand-parenting, and reassures those who do it without skipping over the difficulties . . . She is a reliable advisor."

—*Publishers Weekly*

"A page-turner . . . Don't be deterred by the title; it's good reading for both generations."

—*The Boston Globe*

"On the fine art of being a grandparent, Eda LeShan really shines, suggesting that tolerance is contagious and can work for both grand-parent and grandchild."

—*BookPage* (Nashville, TN)

GRANDPARENTING IN A CHANGING WORLD

WORLD

Eda LeShan

Newmarket Press
New York

For Wendy, who made me a grandmother.

10 9 8 7 6 5 4 3 2 1

Library of Congress Cataloging-in-Publication Data
LeShan, Eda J.
Grandparenting in a changing world / Eda LeShan.
p. cm.
Inciudes bibliographical references.
ISBN 1-55704-175-X hardcover
ISBN 1-55704-307-8 paperback
1. Grandparenting. 2. Grandparent and child. I. Title.
HQ759.9.L45 1993
306.874'5—dc20   93-24988
CIP

QUANTITY PURCHASES
Companies, professional groups, clubs, and other organizations may qualify for
special terms when ordering quantities of this title. For information, write
Special Sales, Newmarket Press, 18 East 48th Street, New York, NY 10017,
or call (212) 832-3575.

Book design by M. J. DiMassi
Manufactured in the United States of America

Contents

ACKNOWLEDGMENTS

So many people gave me so many stories that I can only mention a few of them; grateful thanks go to Freda Gillis, Bella Grossman, Sadie Hofstein, Rhiannon Jackson, Ruth Karter, Robin Kline, and Jean Kotkin.

Special thanks for encouragement beyond the call of duty to Susie Cohen and Phyllis Wender, to my editor, Keith Hollaman, who truly allowed me free reign, and to Shirley Marcus for her excellent care of the manuscript.

My gratitude to Leah Davidson, M.D., for seeing me through from a stroke to a finished book.

And, as always, my love and gratitude to the man who has supplied the "Go, girl, go!" for forty-nine years.

I am especially indebted to Edith S. Engel, who has supplied her expertise as an advocate of grandparents' rights and many other complex issues.

A grandmother is a lady who has no children of her own. She likes other people's little girls.

A grandfather is a man-grandmother. He goes for walks with the boys, and they talk about fishing and tractors and things like that.

Grandmothers don't have to do anything except be there. They're old so they shouldn't play hard or run. It is enough if they drive us to the shops where the pretend horse is, and have lots of dimes ready. Or if they take us for walks, they should never say, "Hurry up," but they should slow down past things like pretty leaves and caterpillars.

It is better if they don't typewrite or play cards except with us.

They don't have to be smart, only answer questions like "Why don't dogs like cats?" or "How come God isn't married?"

They don't talk baby talk like visitors do because it's too hard to understand. When they read to us they don't skip or mind if it is the same story again.

Everyone should try to have one—especially if you don't have television because Grandmas are the only grown-ups who have got time.

—BY AN UNKNOWN THIRD-GRADER

1

Grandparents in a Changing World

I REMEMBER VERY CLEARLY the day my grandchild was born—following a night of great anxiety. When Rhiannon finally arrived more than thirty hours later, she turned out to be almost twelve pounds, and my daughter was pretty wounded. I remember the sleepless night and then the relief when it was over, and my thinking on first seeing her was that this child was too big for the backpack I'd bought. I remember cleaning out my daughter's refrigerator and cooking her meals and getting terribly tired, but I don't recall sensing that my life had changed forever. I called friends and family, and I thought Rhiannon was adorable, but my daughter was not at all comfortable about my holding the baby. She wanted me as a housekeeper.

I felt rejected and hurt until I remembered a story a friend of mine had told me some months before. She said, "I was sure Janet would want me to come and stay with her when Brian was born. I didn't dare to make any appointments for the last two weeks of the month; I kept a bag packed for a quick departure. It was Janet's first baby and we have had a very close relationship. And then she called and said she didn't want me to come; she and her husband, Andy, needed time alone to bond with the baby. I knew this was "the new thing" and I accepted it, but of course was longing to see the baby. A week later Janet called, crying, hysterical—I should come immediately. I guess they had bonded enough and were ready for help!"

I know many cases where both grandparents participated in the birth of a grandchild; sometimes grandparents will resist visiting at once, acknowledging that a daughter-in-law will want her own family. Some new grandparents live too far away or aren't well enough to help. But whatever the circumstances, the birth of the first grandchild does change our lives. Arthur Kornhaber* summed it up succinctly: "Every time a child is born a grandparent is born, too."

Not until I started to write this book did a dramatic revelation come to me. That fateful night and day, eleven years ago, changed my life forever: I would be a grandparent for the rest of my life. I was no longer just a wife and mother and worker. In that miracle of birth I had become a grandparent. It is only now, looking back with some experience and perspective, that I see the full dramatic significance of a role that changes one's life irrevocably. And the longer I have been a grandmother, the more I have realized how complex and challenging this role is.

Part of the complexity is that most of us were unprepared for being grandparents, today, now. How can we learn this new role when our own experiences may have been quite different as grandchildren? Probably just before or during World War II; before atomic bombs; before the massive population explosion;

*Arthur Kornhaber, M.D., and Kenneth Woodward, *Grandparents, Grandchildren: A Vital Connection* (Garden City, N.Y.: Anchor Press/Doubleday, 1981.

before environmental hazards, cities of fear—and perhaps most dramatic of all, before the women's movement, all of which have made enormous changes.

My grandfather worked six days a week in a music store. My grandmother was a homemaker until her death (although she'd been a schoolteacher before she married).

My grandmother was very sure of herself. She scolded me when she felt I was naughty, she cooked all my favorite delicacies when I was sick, and she played games with me. The world we shared was safe and quiet. The big excitement was when the iceman came or when we went to the butcher's and I could slide around on the sawdust floor. We lived on a quiet street, and home and family were the center of my universe. My exposure to the media meant I listened to "Uncle Don" on the radio. I never went to a movie until I was twelve, with Aunt Lillie—*Sunny Side Up*, a romantic musical. I never ate in a restaurant until I was twelve, except once in a while at my Uncle Benny's delicatessen.

My grandmother played pinochle one afternoon a week, with her mother and sisters. That was her entertainment.

Even with a maid, my grandmother shopped, cooked, cleaned, boiled cereal overnight, washed clothes in a tub on the stove, was in the kitchen for eight or more hours a day.

I am an "old grandma," so my memories are surely different from younger grandparents whose childhood world may have been much closer to the world of their grandchildren. But the pace of change has been so rapid that all of us probably experience many differences in our role as grandparents.

I felt my grandparents loved me unconditionally. They had time for me. My grandfather had a dog I loved. He was named "Grumpy," but I can't imagine why—he was as sweet as he could be. I wheeled him around in my doll carriage and later went on long walks with Grumpy and my grandfather. We fed him ice cream cones. We often passed a garden where my grandfather would show me that pansies had faces. He made up stories, gave them each a name. The family, children, and grandchildren were the focuses of my grandparents' lives.

My father's mother didn't speak a word of English. I could tell from her eyes that she loved me, and she would hand me a handkerchief with nuts and raisins in it. She also cooked wonderful meals, and I guess I must have assumed that the world of her seven children, the grandchildren, the sharing of ritual holidays, would just go on forever, unchanging. We couldn't speak to each other except through hugs and smiling, but it seems to me now that our language barrier was less of a problem than mine, in dealing with the language of my granddaughter! Each year I seem to need new definitions of words such as "like" and "cool" and "awesome" and "bad" and "in your face" and so many more.

I guess I always assumed I'd be the same kind of grandparent as my grandparents. But I'm not, and neither are most of my contemporaries. What happened?

Both my mother's and father's families were big, extended. We all lived near each other. If children got noisy or bored or obstreperous there were dozens of aunts and uncles and cousins to take care of us, discipline us, entertain us.

Edith S. Engel, who is a specialist in the field of grandparents' rights (and who is one of the aunts I played with) has written a clear and touching description (edited for this book) of her memories of her grandmother and when her mother became a grandmother:

"To Grandmother's House . . ."

I remember my maternal grandma very vividly.

Grandparents' Day was not even a gleam in Hallmark's eye; nevertheless, the celebration of my Grandma Frances took place

4

not once a year but, like clockwork, each Sunday afternoon year-round.

To Grandma's house trooped her seven daughters and two sons, their husbands and wives, and their broods, totaling some twenty-five, give or take a few victims of tonsillitis or grippe.

Each of the seven sisters brought a specialty of her own house—freshly baked bread, chicken soup, pot roast, roast duck, potato dumplings, grated beets with horseradish, creamed spinach, sauerkraut with apples and caraway seeds, compote of mixed fruits, chocolate yeast cake, apple strudel, and lemon meringue pie. Grandma inevitably provided large cut-glass bowls of raisins and nuts for the grandchildren, and a bottle of pre-Prohibition schnapps for the men that they drank straight from cut-glass jiggers.

Grandma sat erectly in her carved, solid oak, highbacked chair, a black velvet ribbon around her neck, her snow-white hair piled atop her regal head like a diadem. She didn't talk very much to us grandchildren, but when she deigned to address a word or two to any one of us, and smiled with the delivery, it was like being knighted. No doubt about it—she was "The Matriarch."

The generations ate apart. The "children," ranging in age from twenty to six or seven, traditionally ate at a large kitchen table extended by ironing boards resting precariously on top of the backs of chairs. The largest of the grandchildren sat on the seats of those chairs to anchor the makeshift table. The food was superb, undoubtedly the last word in cholesterol (who knew or cared then?), salt, and calories.

Like geese after stuffing, we were dismissed to play outside barring a blizzard, hurricane, or thunderstorm. Our mothers cleaned up in postsurgical fashion under Grandma's watchful eye. When she was satisfied that nothing had been broken, all stowed away properly according to the rules of her house, leftovers in her enormous icebox, and the dishes washed and dried, she would summon my mother and one of her sons or a son-in-law to her card room for her beloved pinochle game.

Since I was young and sickly, and also a "mama's baby," I spent many Sunday afternoons at my mother's elbow as she played pinochle.

When my mother became a grandmother, like a fireman she'd be on call if one of her grandchildren had tonsillitis, a bellyache, or a sty, let alone the typical childhood diseases. It seemed to me Mama looked forward to being with her grandchildren so much that she'd have a pot of chicken soup, with all the vegetables prepared, in the corner of the refrigerator, always primed for an SOS from a parent or a plaintive entreaty from the patient. It didn't matter if it was a cinder in the eye or a reaction from too many rides on a carousel.[†]

As a former elementary school teacher, her larder of stories, songs, nursery rhymes, and games for kids of all ages and incapacities was as available as her culinary stock. And when those grandchildren visited on an afternoon, there was always a bountiful offering of homemade French chocolates with sprinkles, almond crescents, ice cream parfaits, and Charlotte Russes. For insurance, she had store-bought chocolate kisses, chocolate licorice, and Turkish taffy. To satisfy the adults there were always large bowls of fresh fruit. And inevitably there were large cut-glass bowls of assorted nuts and raisins. She never sent her grandchildren out to play, but played with them, not pinochle, but jacks, which she mastered as a child, and Ping-Pong, a skill acquired past sixty. She was incredibly good at both, and the kids adored her.

Now it's my turn at being a grandmother of four, whose ages range from twenty and sixteen to twelve and nine. Visits are not on a regular basis: There are scheduled commitments; parents' jobs; extracurricular activities; homework; and, of course, friends to be with. Magnetized on the door and sides of my refrigerator are drawings, cards, letters, and poems of my grandchildren's authorship, so that I visit with them in effect every time I approach the refrigerator. We talk on the phone more than we see each other. Fortunately for me, I can spend related, happy times with them.

And, like my grandmother and my mother before me, there is always a full bowl of raisins and nuts. I'm not really superstitious, but I wish I'd kept those cut-glass bowls.

[†]What *I*, as one of the grandchildren, remember best was the ecstasy of Nesselrode pudding when I was sick.

Something in me longs to ask my aunt for more stories, and to remember more about my experiences with other grandparents. For me and for them life was simpler, less frustrating. I can't help but feel some sense of loss, regret, but to be successful grandparents, we have to bring ourselves up short and face today's world.

A friend of mine asked her almost-six-year-old grandson what he would like for his birthday. Without a moment's hesitation he said, "A Swiss Army knife." She was shocked by this response and wanted to know why he would want a knife, and he replied, "Because kids on the school bus have knives." His mother also reported that his language development had taken quite a turn, with his asking her what was "a fucking bitch," which he had heard a child on his bus call the bus driver. He seemed to know what "stupid jerk" meant, and that had become his favorite expression.

This is surely a new world for grandparents! We have been ricocheting from wall to wall as we try to figure out how to stay close to grandchildren who seem to have come from some other planet and who speak and behave in ways we find very strange and upsetting. When I heard about this young child, living in a family with excellent values and civilized relationships, I was reminded anew of the challenges we face.

When my daughter was eighteen, she moved into her own apartment with her boyfriend. For many years before this event occurred I had been pretty hysterical—feeling powerless and frightened by the newly liberated attitudes toward premarital sexuality. I adjusted over the years, but it was my mother who taught me how to be a grandmother in today's world. Despite her strict Victorian background, her virginity until marriage, and her faithfulness in marriage, she made a remarkable decision: In spite of a severe heart condition, she walked slowly up to the fifth-floor walk-up where my daughter lived. She brought gifts of a coffeepot, some dishes, and silverware. We had a tea party. Why did she do it, when everything in her background made her so uneasy, so anxious about this new pattern of behavior? She said, "It's simple. I love Wendy; she's my *grandchild*. Nothing must stand in the way of our relationship."

We are faced with so many things that don't come easily or naturally: the sexual revolution; the women's movement, forever changing the roles of men and women; noisy, dirty, frightening, crime-ridden cities; overpopulation and increasing destruction of the resources of the earth; grandchildren who wonder if there will even be a world for them to live in when they grow up. Incredible! Terrible!

Grandchildren living through the awful trauma of divorce; grandchildren in single-parent homes. Grandchildren whose parents both work full-time and where family living becomes frenetic, stressful; where family members lose touch with each other as pressures from the outside world impinge more and more on time together.

We see our grandchildren struggling with learning pressures we probably never experienced, or at least not to the same degree. More children failing, more childhood illnesses that once only happened to adults—ulcers, colitis, migraines. We have virtually wiped out diphtheria and polio, but the new diseases come from stress and can be just as frightening.

We fear for our grandchildren's lives—crime in the streets, food poisoned by chemicals, pollution in the air they breathe, the water they drink. And while it is possible it happened as much or more in earlier generations, we were usually ignorant of child abuse, sexual or otherwise.

Life stresses have become so much more intense as we find it more and more difficult to solve social problems that we feel powerless, despairing, and fearful in ways I know I never was before. I cannot recall ever hearing of anyone having flashbacks after some potentially bad experience did not happen. But that is what has happened to me.

One early Sunday morning I took my visiting nine-year-old granddaughter to the Museum of the City of New York at 103rd Street and Fifth Avenue. We arrived at ten o'clock, but found the gates locked. A man who was sweeping the steps told us the museum would not open that day—in fact, it would be closed for some time due to a fire and necessary repairs. We were both disappointed and decided to try another museum, on the West Side. It was a pleasant, sunny, summer day, and I suggested we walk through Central Park and feed the pigeons and squirrels some popcorn we had with us.

We entered the park at 103rd Street. Very quickly I realized that the park was quite deserted, and as we continued to walk without seeing anyone, I began to panic—something that had never happened to me before in the park. My granddaughter looks about fourteen years old and is a gorgeous, blue-eyed blonde. I suddenly was terrified that something terrible might happen to us. I remembered a movie with Sophia Loren about walking with an adolescent daughter along a road after World War II and a group of soldiers raping both of them; the trauma to the child and the guilt and pain of the mother made for a haunting, terrifying movie. All of a sudden I visualized this happening to my granddaughter—a gang of wild boys finding us utterly alone and attacking her.

I could not believe I was having such thoughts. Nothing like this had ever happened to me before. I was flooded by wild panic, and, at the same time, was shocked and ashamed. This was my park. I had played in the park almost every day during my childhood. I had been riding the Central Park Carousel for more than sixty years (and still do at frequent intervals). I knew exactly which hill my cousin and I had flown down on our sleds. I had played Tarzan games on the rocks near 63rd Street.

And as a teenager, my friends and I had walked through the park at any time of the day or evening without ever being afraid—never even thinking of the possibility of danger. My park, my playground, and here I was terrified—urging my grand-daughter to walk a little faster, telling her we'd find more squirrels farther along, looking desperately for other people, and realizing that the dumbest thing I could have done was to enter the park so early on a Sunday morning in the very area in which terrible things had recently happened.

Suddenly there was a bunch of teenage boys laughing, shouting, coming toward us. I felt sheer terror, but they went by without looking at us. Then I saw a black man coming toward us—nicely dressed, carrying a briefcase, the sort of person I would never have noticed before, and surely he would never have evoked the slightest anxiety. I, who had fought for civil rights from the time I was a young kid, who had been truly color-blind.

I fell on the way home along Central Park West—tripped on a curb. We were running for a bus and I thought it was an accident. Since then I have wondered if it hadn't been a way of punishing myself for my terror, and as I have contemplated this experience over and over again, I realize that the worst terror, the most unbearable fear, was not our walk through the park but what has happened to me—the end of faith and trust in the world and the people around me.

Did we ever hear of "househusbands"? Were we as aware as we are today of the effects of drugs on our grown children, our grandchildren?

I remember being very shocked at the age of fifteen when I read a book that reported that some jazz musicians "smoked pot" (I don't remember exactly what the word for marijuana was back then). I could hardly believe such a thing. As grand-parents, all of us live in a nightmare of terror about the drugs, the early sexual experimentation, the dangers of disease (as terrifying as AIDS), feeling helpless to protect our grandchildren.

Many of us were working women; many of us had some household help. Almost all of us had husbands who were there, even though few cooked or washed dishes. I never hoped that my husband would do household chores. After all, my own father had never changed a diaper. But Larry was partner and companion, and separation and divorce seemed very remote. We only knew one couple among our peers who divorced while raising young children. But divorce is now a reality for 50 percent of the population of young and middle-aged parents who are raising our grandchildren. I sometimes think that the fear of this ever-present possibility, and watching from the sidelines as it happens, scares us almost as much as it does the children.

Of course, whenever things change, there are some pleasant surprises. I was at first shocked when my very traditional mother-in-law fell in love with a man younger than my husband and had an affair in her seventies and eighties. A widowed aunt flowered anew after caring for a sick husband for fifteen years; now, at seventy-nine, she travels around the world with her boyfriend. What all of us have had to do is change our definition of "family." Tradition is gone, but loving and caring are still the heart of the matter. A family is a single mother and child; a family is two homosexuals who have lived together for forty years; a family is ten young couples living in an apartment building and who share child caring, take responsibilities, and cooperate.

Change in itself is neither "bad" nor "good." We constantly need to examine, reevaluate, choose. But first we need to become more acutely attuned to what the changes are. For example, not only have the times changed, but now grandparents come in more shapes and sizes, more variations of roles and interests than ever before. We have far more choice than our grandparents had, especially grandmothers; hopefully men are beginning to have more options as well, but it's coming much more slowly.

I swim almost every day, mostly to control increasing problems of arthritis and for the continuing struggle to recover from a stroke. There are lots of grandmothers in the pool. One looks like an Olympic athlete; another looks twenty years younger after a face-lift and new hair color. Some seem older because of gray hair and wrinkles. Some are working women, some spend every afternoon at poolside playing cards. I know several who volunteer at a nursing home across the street. Some talk about shopping, some about politics, some about investments, others about what ails them.

If you happen to have a chance to see some old movies from the thirties and forties, it is startling to see what grandparents looked like, even glamorous stars such as Irene Dunne and Bette Davis. Makeup gave them wrinkles, white hair was in a bun, they walked with a cane. As I got older and tried to figure out what age they were supposed to be, I discovered they were supposed to be fifty or sixty! We rarely see this stereotypical grandma even in their seventies or eighties now.

There are enormous differences in the functions of grandparents. I have a friend who sees her grandson at least three times a week. He comes to visit her while his parents are working. They live a few blocks away. Grandma has Central Park across from her apartment building. I'm so jealous of her. I have always lived three hundred miles away from my granddaughter; I never was close enough to live through all the miraculous stages of her growth. I have other friends who only see their grandchildren once or twice a year, who live three thousand miles apart.

Some of our sons and daughters are eager for us to play a significant part in the lives of our grandchildren; some have old grievances against us and don't trust their parents alone with the grandchildren. Some adult children and their parents agree on childraising methods and philosophy; some are far apart.

The more choices there are, the more complex and difficult life becomes. More anxieties, more confusion, uncertainty. The more choices grandparents have, the more interesting life becomes, but the roles become more and more complicated. More adventure hopefully, but also more confusion.

Some grandparents are delighted by grandchildren who are smarter and more sophisticated than earlier generations. I tremble at the prospect of children with no time for childhood. In 1965 I wrote a book titled *The Conspiracy Against Childhood.* The gist of it was what I saw as the terrible new pressures on children to grow up too fast, academically and emotionally. I was sure they would become psychologically crippled, and it breaks my heart that my crystal ball was so accurate. Our grandchildren are being rushed through childhood as if it were a race that had to be won by twenty-one, instead of seeing growth as a lifetime of growing and learning.

I listen to my grandchild talk about what she is learning in school. At eight she was doing long division, at ten she could use a computer. She had tests in grammar in third grade. The math she does now I didn't hear about until I was in high school, and I failed grammar entirely in sixth grade and have almost no idea what sentence structure is all about, although I have written almost thirty books. My grammar comes from reading a lot. I'm very short on specific facts but I can reason, I know where to go for information. I couldn't do an algebra problem if someone stood over me with a gun, but I have had a creative life and I understand a lot about human beings. I wonder if my granddaughter will be allowed to dream, explore, experiment—

understand that failure is an avenue for learning, that the secret of a happy life is the discovery of one's own most profound wishes and talents.

The drugs, the alcohol, the sexual experimentation, the anorexia, the suicides among teenagers all represent what happens if we treat children like machines that we can stuff with facts. Play becomes a luxury instead of a necessity. I see a grandfather at the swimming pool with a four-year-old granddaughter, so delighted to be with him until he says, "Now no fooling around, you have to learn to swim!" Caught in the panic about learning, I hear a grandmother say, at the same pool, when a grandson is terrified of diving into the deep end, "I came all the way from California to see you swim and dive. What's the matter today?" What is probably the matter is that love is so conditional, dependent on performance, that skills already mastered become impossible to demonstrate.

What we need to remember is that our grandchildren need reassurances, comfort, support from us. They already have too many fears; they are not as hopeful about the future. There is far less stability in their lives. They all worry about parents' divorcing. Too many of them find their parents worrying about losing jobs, losing homes, sleeping in cars and shelters. While we lived through the Depression and two world wars, we were idealists, we didn't lose hope. People seemed to stick together; there was less panic than there is today.

My father went to a free college. My college tuition was less than a thousand dollars a year. Life was hard, but we believed in the future.

When I was young, I looked to leaders who were compassionate, concerned: Roosevelt, La Guardia, Governor Lehman. They were all Democrats, like my parents. Being liberal meant worrying about Sacco and Vanzetti, about race relations; all we had to do to make things better and fairer was for the middle class to join the NAACP! Now I hear liberal-bashing every time I turn on the radio. In addition, there is such rage, such hopeless despair by the millions of poor and disenfranchised. I feel like the enemy—helpless, powerless to do anything.

We worry about the stresses on our adult children. "I think my daughter is killing herself," another grandmother tells me. "She works all day, goes shopping, cooks the meals, helps with the homework, takes my grandchildren to doctors and dentists and music lessons, goes to PTA meetings, God knows what else. She'll be dead before she's forty!"

Lots of the things that trouble us are strange, different. "I try hard," one grandmother tells me, "but I can't get used to my son-in-law staying home and taking care of the grandchildren." A grandfather says, "I try to keep my mouth shut, but every day I worry about my grandson walking home from school in a tough, dangerous neighborhood. I lived there myself, but it was different, safe—we all knew each other."

We know that men, women, and children have all been greatly influenced and affected by the women's revolution of the past thirty years, but I don't recall ever reading or hearing anything about the influence on grandparents.

One man told me he was having a sixty-fifth-birthday party with all his children and grandchildren around his dining-room table. Arthur got up to make a speech honoring his wonderful wife, who had gone to a great deal of trouble to make his favorite meal—some very fancy gourmet dish. He announced, bragging, "I want you to know that although it is very hard work, my wife prepared this beautiful dish all by herself." His five-year-old granddaughter at the other end of the table piped up, "Why didn't you help her?"

That is the voice of the new child; in her world, men help, or even do the cooking. Although my grandmother spent probably eight to ten hours a day preparing her wonderful dishes, not only for parties but also for every day of the week, it would never have occurred to me that my grandpa should help her! He went to the store, and she took care of the home. Arthur later told me, "It was a shock, but we all laughed. But I must tell you I feel much less uncomfortable about the fact that my son is an equal homemaker and parent with my daughter-in-law. I had to face the fact that the relations between the sexes are totally different from my own early experience." I asked him if he now helped his wife. He laughed and said, "She'd kill me if I came into the kitchen when she's cooking!" Even if we can't or don't want to change our ways, we need to become more aware of the fact that in relation to the male and female roles of today, we are dinosaurs.

One of the most dramatic changes has been family mobility. All our ancestors (except Native American grandparents) came to this country as immigrants, and there were long separations as family members made the often difficult and dangerous trips. Certainly those brave pioneers who moved westward left relatives and family behind. Most were desperate for a new life, and the price of survival was often painful, but they knew it was worthwhile. But today we have a new and different kind of challenge. Most of us grew up on one street in one town; all or most of our relatives lived in the same city. As a child, all my close relatives lived within one hour's travel at most; our grandparents were available to us, we visited constantly. Rare movies, no television, little eating in restaurants. It was the family that met almost every Sunday, all holidays, in sickness and in health. We began to move away from our center as we became adults—slowly, hardly noticeably. Not so our children and grandchildren, who move freely, easily, by plane, choose to live three thousand miles away, are moved by large corporations frequently, move three hundred, five hundred, maybe only seventy-five or a hundred miles away but are now so much busier, have so many distractions and new activities, and the expense of travel is prohibitive.

What I have seen happen is the blood relationships becoming less important, new ties taking place. Our grandchildren, living with a single parent, speak of "Aunt Frances," "Uncle Charlie" when speaking about neighbors, friends of their parent; families of former strangers help each other in the ways that family members once did. With families split apart, other relationships take their place, with substitute grandparents, aunts, uncles, and cousins. Churches and other social organizations now often match older people who live far from their grandchildren to foster families, a creative but not entirely satisfactory solution.

One of my deep regrets is that almost nobody writes letters anymore. Telephone calls are what all but a few prefer. Mine was a writing family—we even wrote letters to each other while we were in the same house! I suppose there are many people who find a sense of real contact through telephone calls, but no matter what AT&T tries to tell me, I can't make an emotional connection on a telephone but can pour my heart out in a letter. My grandnieces and grandnephews don't write letters.

There are several hundred relatives my daughter doesn't know at all; my granddaughter knows only the immediate family. When I was a child, I felt I was part of a clan, warmly surrounded by people who loved me because I belonged to them. I feel sad about this no longer existing.

Becoming more flexible, open-minded, having a capacity to deal with change is a good thing. But it is far from the whole story. Grandparents, in the absence of the social institutions that once demanded civilized behavior, have their work cut out for them. Our grandchildren are hungry for our love and approval, but also for standards being set.

Some things, however, remain constant despite the tumult. It is still possible—and necessary—to tell that six-year-old he can't have a knife and that we don't approve of name-calling. What has not changed one iota is a role grandparents have had all along: to be on the side of what is absolutely right. Moral values, ethical human relationships remain our business. We are against people hurting each other.

It gets tougher when a grandchild smokes, or seems headed for what we consider too early sexual experimentation, or enjoys the most terrible sounds we have ever heard (at deafening decibels) and calls it music.

Whatever the age of the upsetting, sometimes frightening behavior, one thing is absolutely essential: Whatever we say to try to explain a different point of view, we must always make it clear we love the grandchild unconditionally. Secondly, we can be acceptable role models only if we try, as they say, "to understand where they are 'coming from.' " We need to be good listeners and show we are trying to communicate with them, and that beneath changes in behavior there are still common bonds. Laughter and loving and listening are the talents we need as we try to play our important roles in the lives of our grandchildren.

One grandmother told me, "I feel I have succeeded beyond even my own wildest expectations. My thirteen-year-old granddaughter now has streaks of purple hair with a little orange thrown in. She is also a militant enthusiast for the women's movement and has already assured me that she is going to graduate school and will be a professional woman. She tells me this expecting me to be shocked, disapproving, because I am a full-time homemaker. 'Not at all,' I said, 'I feel so fortunate some dean in college will discourage you from becoming a doctor or lawyer if you have purple and orange hair!' She laughed and hugged me."

The central challenge to grandparents today is to hang in there, no matter what the challenges may be.

❧ 2 ❧

The Unfinished Business Between Adult Children and Their Parents

OUR GRANDCHILDREN ARE not born in a vacuum. Long before they arrive, it is a good idea to increase our awareness of the past we have shared with our children—the potential parents of our future grandchildren.

One inevitable issue is a question of power. Once we had total control over our children. We have had less and less to say about how they conduct their lives as they have reached maturity.

Hopefully, if we've done our job well, they will have made their own choices about work, friends, love. They choose where they want to live, a style of life—everything from their stereo set to magazine subscriptions to wine to sports activities. We may have been pleased with how they "turned out," or we may be mildly or deeply troubled, but by and large most parents learn (often the hard way!) to practice a hands-off policy (unless there are signs of serious psychological problems, when we will want to try to encourage seeking expert help).

Everything changes when our children become parents. After all, we think, this we know more about than they do! One grandmother, facing the truth, told me, "The worst thing about being a grandmother is we're not in control!" We surely are not! And we'd better not be—except under the most unusual circumstances. As a shift in roles is coming to a final culmination, we need to spend time trying to discover if there is some hidden agenda between us and our children that may cause minor or more serious difficulties.

What was happening when we became parents? Were we young and unsure of ourselves so that the baby became anxious? Was the child an "accident," who threw us off course for a while? Maybe some frustration and resentment was some of the background music. Or had we been longing for a child for a long time, so that the earliest climate of life for the child was great joy and exuberance?

I was a damned good nursery school teacher when my daughter arrived on the scene. There was nothing a three- or four-year-old could do that I didn't feel confident to deal with admirably. But a tiny, colicky baby? Panic! One of my earliest memories is of my husband, Larry, coming home from work, finding both the baby and me crying hysterically, and his holding one of us on each shoulder. Before that, both my parents had rushed from New York to Chicago because I was so terribly frightened of this tiny, miserable creature.

I look back now, forty-three years later, and I feel so guilty I wasn't a better mother in the beginning. But, then, I watched in wonder and joyful amazement my daughter Wendy's capacity to be the most nurturing, adoring mother from the moment my grandchild was born. What luck—I hadn't ruined her life by my ineptitude! But the places where we made mistakes as parents do crop up in painful ways.

For example, also probably because I was such a terrific nursery school teacher, I was a casual mother; I wanted Wendy to have a wonderful time playing hard, getting dirty, not worrying about getting finger paint on her clothes. So I sent her to nursery school in secondhand overalls and sensible play clothes, never dresses. We later learned that Wendy felt she was Cinderella! It was a shock—she was always dressed beautifully for parties and company, but that didn't seem to be what she was picking up. My granddaughter, of course, was impeccably outfitted, nursery school or not! When Rhiannon was about two and a half, I took her for a walk along a wooded road. We played a game I played with all the children in my classes. We would look for grasses and weeds that resembled vegetables and play "store." Big, wide leaves were spinach; there was one weed that looked just like a carrot top. We decided little stones could be eggs and bigger stones could be meat. When we arrived back at my daughter's home, having had a wonderful time, Wendy was furious with me. The woods were dirty, dogs "did their business there," there might be red ants, Rhiannon's hands were filthy, heaven only knew what germs she might have picked up; she was thoroughly scrubbed immediately!!

I was hurt and angry. I figured I wasn't an idiot; I'd raised a child who was now a healthy young woman—what was this all about? I was a casual mother in most departments, never worried much about dirt or germs. What I finally figured out was that, during her early childhood, Wendy must have felt insecure about my easygoing ways. That may not be the correct explanation, but it was helpful all the same. I had a plausible reason for her behavior. Maybe I had been too laid-back, too permissive, and she was afraid for her child's life!

Many grandparents have told me they feel that their children are more suspicious and disapproving of our relationship with their children than we were when our parents became grandparents. I doubt this—I think it's probably poor memory. But each generation brings into grandparenthood a multitude of mixed feelings.

Some situations were more clear-cut. I wasn't casual about everything. On Saturday mornings when I was a child, my mother often came into my bedroom, screamed at me about "the mess," swept the toys off the shelves, and told me to clean up. I remember my silent prayer after she left the room: "Please, God, I'm never going to be this mean to a child of mine!"

Of course, twenty-five years later, I was behaving like my mother. I couldn't seem to control myself—I hated what I was doing. Fortunately for Wendy, her father was very casual (the understatement of the century) about neatness. "Come on, Wendy," he'd say, "your mother is crazy this morning. Let's go to the park."

Wendy was much better at this aspect of motherhood than I, but once in a while there would be a crazy streak in her as she surveyed the chaos in her daughter's room. But the third generation was moving along at a more rational level.

We were also very casual about schoolwork. (I haven't changed my mind one iota on this subject.) Wendy felt we should have been stricter, set definite limits. She is more realistic than we were. She supervises homework, is concerned about grades, sets a clear goal about college. I guess we were so much more concerned with her feelings that we didn't help her to achieve. Somewhat guilty, we watched her being so much more disciplined about her child's schoolwork.

The struggle during adolescence was, to put it mildly, pretty hysterical. We were parents of a teenager during the sexual revolution, when smoking pot was the "thing to do" and dressing outrageously a necessity. (Now most people have followed the flower children into sandals, men with long hair, earrings, and torn jeans!) My adjustment was very rough—Larry was more comfortable even when our daughter was walking barefoot on Broadway (talk about germs!) in a Columbia University nightshirt with a flower painted on her cheek. We were both naive—plain stupid—about sex and worried ourselves sick about alcohol and drugs.

Meanwhile, Wendy kept her head when all around her was chaos. As a result, she is completely comfortable—eager, happy—about her daughter's approaching adolescence.

Once, standing at the sink with me, cleaning vegetables for supper, when she was about twenty, I asked, "Wendy, how come you felt so free to rebel, to experiment, when your mother was a holdover from the Victorian age and so uptight?" Her answer was full of brilliant insight. She said, "I didn't listen to your conscious, I listened to your unconscious." (My adolescence passed with absolutely no adventures!)

I mention these few of many examples of past events only to indicate that generation after generation we pass along attitudes, behavior, some parenting that we are proud of, plenty of things we wish we'd done better. Before the arrival of the grandchildren it's a good idea to communicate about the past and get some perspective on what was going on.

When I was in my twenties, I started what turned out to be about fifty years of on-again, off-again psychotherapy. Not knowing any better (the therapist should have), I became very hostile toward my mother. Later I learned that the first part of therapy is for exploring the hurts, but that the second, more important half, is understanding, compassion, and forgiveness. My mother's been dead for more than twenty years; how I wish I could tell her how much I loved her! I am awash in guilt for frightening her, hurting her.

Wendy has certainly confronted us occasionally with things she has learned about herself that show us up as fallible, imperfect parents. But we did not react with panic, as my mother had. Wendy was much more forgiving. When a friend asked her what it was like being raised by two psychologists, she answered, "They made as many mistakes as all parents make, but I always knew they were trying to grow and change." We were home free!

Before a grandchild is even conceived, it's the better part of wisdom to sit down with the young couple and ask questions about how they felt growing up. How have these experiences colored their thoughts about being parents? And more important than the questions, listen to their answers! It's too late to change the past—guilt will solve nothing for us nor anger for them. Insight and communication are what are needed to settle old business.

At a family party a younger cousin, Frank, said to me, "I moved as far away from my mother as I could get. She smothered me." His mother was my aunt; I adored her. She was always there for me when I needed her. I remembered that she commuted every day, at dawn, to teach in the city, so her children could have the advantages of life in the suburbs. Frank doesn't remember that. It made me both angry and sad, now that my aunt is dead and I miss her so much.

My daughter, today forty-three, recently talked about how deep her hurt had been when she was unceremoniously thrown out of a supposedly progressive school because of learning problems; nobody had then heard of dyslexia. I heard a depth of pain I had not fully understood. It made me feel I should have raised more hell with the stupid school.

I called a friend and she sounded very depressed. She told me, "Karen came in from Dallas with the kids, to visit us for a week. She spent most of the time telling me all the things I had done that were wrong when she was a child. Not Harry, you understand, just me. She's in therapy now and it's as if she doesn't have a single happy memory." Whether one's children choose therapy or not, there comes a time when I think it is appropriate to say sweetly but firmly, ENOUGH ALREADY! We will try, of course, not to make the same mistakes with our grandchildren. There is nothing we can do about the old wounds of our children's early life; we can sympathize and work to improve relations, of course, but we cannot go back. I think it's a good idea to make this clear when necessary—when we feel attacked for old business we can't change.

The background agenda often becomes more intense when our children choose (we hope!) life partners. Martha married an African-American. Her background was white, Italian, Catholic. Her mother let it be known she was heartbroken, but she visited her daughter and son-in-law. While she was terrified of the problems they might have to face, she knew there was nothing she could do and that she didn't want to lose her daughter. Martha's father, however, refused to attend the wedding and said he would never speak to his daughter again.

Alfred and Miriam refused to be married by a rabbi because they said they were atheists. They were married by a judge. Alfred's Orthodox parents never acknowledged that they were legally married and refused to see them.

Julia, raised as a Methodist, asked her parents to accept her marriage to a young man who had become a Buddhist. The parents were horrified, and while they saw the couple once in a while, they didn't attend the wedding and never invited them to any family gathering. At Thanksgiving, Julia invited her college-age brother to come to her home instead of their parents', and created a major confrontation and crisis.

In all these cases, differences hit hard at older family values and prejudices, causing tension, disapproval, hurt feelings, rejection, and anger. And too often, babies are born into the crossfire. These are the kinds of issues that we need to try to resolve before grandchildren are born. Whether one likes it or not, it is up to us, as parents, to try to resolve the problems.

Our children who are not yet parents cannot fully understand how important grandparents are to children. In the first full blush of passionate love they often feel quite cavalier about insisting on their right to live their own lives, and to hell with their parents. If we loved and needed our grandparents, we know we mustn't lose these wars.

What we have to learn is that many of our fears are based on attitudes we learned as children, that we are inflexible about some differences. In one case, Alice's parents felt like cutting their throats: A Phi Beta Kappa student with a Ph.D. in ancient history, Alice fell in love with and married a truck driver. Her parents did everything they could think of to dissuade her; they were sure that it was "just sex." What was the good of spending so much money to educate their daughter if she was going to lower herself intellectually? Ten years later, Alice is head of the special studies program in ancient history at a small college; the couple have two young children. As if they had never carried on, Grandma says, "Oh, George is the sweetest person! He encourages Alice in her work, he takes care of the children, he's wonderful to us!" Grandpa says, "George and I have a lot in common. We fish, we go to baseball games, we take the children to the botanical gardens. Imagine—he knows all about the varieties of orchids!"

So much for differences. What we will discover, if we give it half a chance, is that differences in race, religion, economic status, and education are not the important issues. Overall values, attitudes about human relationships, the capacity to change, to compromise are what we ought to be concerned about. When a person says, "Never darken my doorstep again!" he or she is going to be robbed of all the potential joys of grandparenthood.

The majority of parents will still be willing to see their own child, if not their in-law, when the rigidity of feelings are just too intense to overcome right away. A young Chinese-American woman told me, "It hurts me so much to see my parents reject my Jewish husband without even being willing to meet him. And it hurts my husband when I insist I will have to see them alone for the time being. But I feel that they will appreciate how much I love them and eventually they will change their minds. I tell my husband that when I go to see them I am trying to set the stage for a reconciliation."

She's a wise young woman. I think it is helpful if the adult child maintains a relationship with parents, seeing them alone, allowing for time to bring about change. I hope those of you caught in the irrationality of fear and hatred of differences will appreciate a child's love and work harder at changing yourselves.

The almost overwhelming antidote in such situations is the coming of a grandchild. The altogether natural human yearning to see ourselves immortalized, to melt at a toothless smile or at arms held out to us, usually solves the problem—but only in part. Hurt feelings need to be assuaged, discussed, and a genuine open and honest reconciliation must be made. It is necessary for all involved to express their feelings, talk about their background experiences, and offer and accept forgiveness.

"My granddaughter was two years old," Millie told me, "before my son, his wife, my husband, and I were able to sit down and talk about the debacle of their wedding. They wanted a small, intimate wedding in their apartment (where they'd already been living for a year), and we wanted a catered affair with a few hundred guests in a place where nobody had to know they were living together already. It was a disaster. It took three years to be able to laugh about it, and the reason it happened was that that precious grandchild got meningitis and almost died." It's such things that put everything in perspective.

It calls for great sensitivity on our part to understand ourselves and our grown children. It calls for an open mind, a belief in common human needs, and feelings and moral values. Our goal must be to "set the record straight," to make amends where we can, and to acknowledge that we are supposed to be more mature than the young couple and should be patient for them to learn more through their own life experiences. The main thing is to know we all lived full, varied, different lives before we came together to look through the hospital nursery window.

Fortunately, that tiny, adorable little person, with no prejudices, no hidden agenda, has the power to make us see the light.

~ 3 ~

Who Raises the Children?

IF GRANDPARENTS WANT to have a meaningful and constructive role, the first lesson they must learn is that becoming a grandparent is *not* having a second chance at parenthood! The less sure we may be about whether we did a good job as parents, the more likely we are to forget this essential rule.

When I was working as a consultant in a nursery school many years ago, a grandmother rushed into the school on a crisp autumn day and told her grandson's teacher, "Here's a sweater for Josh—I knew my daughter would forget to bring one!"

The issue of who raises the children is the source of considerable conflict, misunderstandings, and a continuing need for honest communication between parents and grandparents.

Grandmothers worry about food—mostly that their daughters must "make the kids eat." Some mothers worry about letting Grandma baby-sit because she gets distracted and doesn't watch the children closely enough in the park. One daughter wrote,

"I grew up in a small town where all the neighbors knew each other. My mother has no understanding of the dangers in a big-city park. She gets talking to other people on the bench and doesn't keep her eye on the playground."

In the past few years many of my friends have told me that they are hardly even allowed to do anything with their grand-children alone—a parent is always in the background. One spoke for all: "It's as if they don't trust us." One mother told me, "My parents are wonderful people but they cannot com-prehend the world the way it is today. They never worried about crime, drugs, sex, even AIDS. They have no idea of the pressure on kids today to grow up too fast. I don't expect them always to understand the crises we go through. All I want is their support—sometimes *we* need comforting!" Other young par-ents, on the other hand, have complained that grandparents never offer to baby-sit—they are always too tired.

Patterns of childraising may have changed so much that par-ents and grandparents may get into serious conflicts. A grand-mother who was raised at a time when "bowel regularity" had been considered an absolute necessity, and who had been given castor oil often as a child, was terribly upset when her grandson didn't have a bowel movement every day. "My mother made such a damn fuss that when we left Steve with her for a week, he became completely constipated and was so backed up when we got home that we had to take him to the pediatrician," his mother told me. "We never paid attention to when he went to the bathroom and there never had been any problem."

When young parents heed our advice, we have a bad habit of thinking they are still "good children." If they reject our opinion, we think they are "bad." Whether they take our advice or criticism or not, we need, for all our sakes, to assume they are simply fulfilling their rights and obligations as parents. It is true that some of their decisions are based on wanting to behave differently with their children because they feel we made mistakes with them.

Maybe we occasionally used corporal punishment; they make it clear they never will. Or we were very permissive and they are stricter. Or we gave them too many sweets and now they may tell us this was bad for them and their children cannot have cookies and cake except on special occasions; we are not to bring any sweets when we visit. I envy my mother; we didn't know much of anything about nutrition when my daughter was young, and Grandma loved to indulge Wendy with goodies. I didn't mind at all—I had not yet realized what a sugaraholic I was. When I became a grandmother I usually agreed with the new awareness about the connection between food and health, but when I took my granddaughter to the theater and it seemed as if every other child in the theater had candy bars and all I had been allowed to bring Rhiannon was a peanut butter sandwich and some raisins, I was extremely frustrated. On this issue I fought back. My daughter relented—on special occasions some indulgences were all right. It came as a shock a few years later, at the circus, to see my granddaughter eating cotton candy! Now I thought my daughter had swung too far to the opposite side! When I expressed surprise, she said, "One has to make exceptions on special occasions!" One for my side. But with more information available to both of us, we are now in tune on the subject of food.

If she had stuck to her guns with no exceptions to the rule, I would have had to accept it, and that is really the issue. It is all right to protest, argue a little, when there are disagreements, but when the chips are down, parents decide about food, clothing, discipline, money, chores, and all the rest of childraising.

One reason for trying to mind our own business most of the time is that there is new information all the time. Grandparents, for example, have a tendency to panic when a child is sick and isn't put to bed immediately. I was shocked when my grand-daughter was walking around, playing on the floor, when she had the flu. A natural reaction; there were no antibiotics when I was a child, and a temperature of 103 degrees was cause for alarm. I remember diphtheria, scarlet fever, and polio most of all, with terror. The crisis scene in *Little Women*, waiting to see if Beth would live or die, was grounds for floods of tears and anguish. Today's children can't imagine what all the fuss was about! This is one of many cases where the younger the grandparents the better, since their own experiences are closer to those of their grandchildren. But even younger grandparents are likely to find some major changes due to progress since their own childhood.

It isn't as if we have to abdicate from concern and caring. Certainly when grandchildren are in our care, we have to make decisions. It seems to me that we have an obligation to raise questions when something important bothers us, especially in the realm of safety, or attitudes and behavior that we feel are setting a pattern for life. We can suggest, call attention to, ex-press a point of view, but at all times making it quite clear that final decisions are in the hands of the parents. The only excep-tion to this is if there are serious pathological problems—child abuse, alcoholism, drugs, mental breakdown—where we must do everything we can do to bring expert help into the situation.

A grandmother wrote me, "I am very concerned about my son and his family. My son is forty, my grandson is nine. He is an only child. I see very little of them, but when I do, my son is always putting down my grandson. This child is doing poorly in school, and his father calls him 'stupid.' My grandson is a beautiful, delightful, accommodating child. I am afraid he will lose his natural enthusiasm. My son had difficulty learning but finally graduated from high school. He works hard at physical labor. His wife is a college graduate and is working toward a master's degree. My son has never been able to take any kind of criticism, so I say nothing. (I am a widow.) But his sarcasm and the way he demeans his child are very upsetting to me."

Sometimes the behavior of a parent may be a way to annoy a grandparent if there is "old business" from childhood. The letter mentions that her son was insecure as a child. It may be that observing that his son has some of the same problems causes the father to be frightened and angry. If the grandson is so delightful and charming, it's hard to imagine that he feels rejected or worthless. What one can do is try to reassure the father as to *his* value as a son and a father, to let him know his mother feels that she may have failed him in some ways and that that makes her sad now. But most of all, Grandma can use her time with her grandson to let him know how much she loves him. She might help him with his schoolwork if together they could have some special adventures in learning, such as going to museums, a zoo, an aquarium, or perhaps one or more of the historic restorations that may be in her area. Encouraging his curiosity, serving as a loving companion may help him to have an easier time with school than his father did.

One grandma has the right idea. She called me up and said, "I want to know if you think what I'm doing is okay. When I see something I don't approve of, I say, 'Listen, kids, I know these are your children and I don't want to interfere. I just want to tell you my opinion. We all understand you don't have to pay any attention to me.'" I told her I thought that was fine. Young parents are far more likely to be willing to listen to suggestions, even criticism, if the background music is respect and knowing the limits of one's authority.

We need to practice the art of guidance without claims, the capacity to make supportive suggestions rather than interfering. Sometimes it's just a matter of the tone of voice or the wording of an opinion. It's the difference between saying, for example,

"That kitchen cabinet is a disaster! How can you get anything done?" as opposed to saying, "I know how hard it is to have a full-time job and run a household. Would it help if I tried to organize these shelves?" It's the difference between saying, "That child is never going to learn how to behave unless you teach her some manners!" as opposed to saying, "Do you feel she's too young to learn to say 'please' or 'thank you'? I know there's a difference of opinion about whether you just teach by example or by reminding."

In some respects, grandparents do make important choices for their grandchildren. I would never give a toy gun to a grandchild—it is a matter of principle to me. If a grandchild were to say, "Mommy and Daddy gave me a toy machine gun for Christmas," I would say, "Your parents have a right to do what they think is right, but sometimes I don't agree with them." One grandmother told me her son-in-law had bought his daughter a doll that is pregnant—I think it was a new and revolutionary Barbie doll. She told me, "My daughter and I thought it was grotesque, but she told me I shouldn't say anything to her husband, and she was quaking when I didn't pay attention but told him that women would feel it was offensive in every way, since the fetus was in a hole in the stomach, there was no evidence of a vagina, and pregnancy and childbirth are too important for such commercialism. He did look angry and asked how children should learn about all this, and I said with good books, pictures, and sex education. My daughter was relieved, and I think she appreciated my using my age and authority in defense of her point of view." However, if both parents had chosen the doll, Grandma might have expressed her opinion privately, without being quite as judgmental. Sometimes parents just simply don't want to hear our opinions at all, and we need to accept that. Everybody has a right to make his or her own mistakes—or, more likely, to improve on us as parents. Instead of feeling insulted, hurt, fearful that our parenting is being fiercely criticized, it is the better part of wisdom to see to it that we have rich, full lives of our own and give as much love as we can to our grandchild in our own way.

We are fortunate if we can remember our own experiences with grandparents, some of whom may still be alive. What were the things we loved most about them? What experiences do we remember with the most pleasure? Hopefully not fights they had with our parents! We wanted a separate, special relationship, not a competition with our parents. What we remember best are playfulness, companionship, TLC when we were sick, private adventures. Very often the best grandparents were the ones most unlike our parents! The rules were different, the activities were special, the range of ideas with which they presented us, added to our lives, did not simply repeat what our parents told us or did. They were the storytellers about the past, they showed us albums, told us about their relatives, their childhood. These are the legitimate functions for grandparents, enough to satisfy our genuine, natural need to participate in our grandchildren's lives.

For many years I had an advice column in *Woman's Day* magazine. A great many of the letters I received had to do with ambivalent feelings between parents and grandparents.

One young mother wrote:

> I have a seven-month-old daughter whom my mother baby-sits while I'm at work. Although I am grateful, I feel my mother overdoes it. I'm afraid my daughter will grow up spoiled and unmanageable. My mother picks her up whenever she cries. I feel her care is being taken completely out of my hands.

Sometimes theories of childraising differ. (I happen to agree that babies should be picked up when they cry.) Sometimes feelings of rivalry occur—a working mother may be jealous of a grandparent spending more time with her child than she can.

Children learn, surely by two or three years, the important difference in the intensity of their relationships with parents and with grandparents. They also understand—often better than the adults—that grandparents are specially designed to spoil grandchildren, and children discover this very early in life. Parents are for loving and helping you grow up; grandparents are for loving. A similar letter reports:

> I have a seventeen-month-old son, and my problem is my mother-in-law. She's a wonderful, giving person, but she just takes over. If my son doesn't finish some food, she will take him into another room to feed him. When he wakes up from a nap, she races me to the room. She calls another pediatrician to check up on what my doctor tells me. We visit her home only occasionally, but she has a crib, high chair, playpen, walker, food, diapers, clothes, toys ready for him. She's happily married and active, but she acts as if her mothering is better than mine. I know you are a firm believer in the importance of grandparents, and I wonder if I'm being oversensitive.

Sometimes grown-ups need limits as much as children do! This mother has every right to insist that certain routines—such as feeding—are areas in which she feels she has to make the decisions. But when Grandma equips her home in ways in which her grandchild will be most comfortable, that seems reasonable to me. Sometimes an oversensitive mother may be feeling she's losing control. But rather than feeling attacked for one's own mothering skills, it may be that Grandma feels that in some ways she failed as a mother and now wants to compensate for that. While insisting that in matters of health and daily routines parents are in charge, it helps if they occasionally ask for help and advice.

Another mother wrote me:

> I am going to have my second child in two months. My mother-in-law is coming to help out. She is a very controlling woman, with old-fashioned ideas about childraising; she believes in spanking, forcing a child to eat, etc. She bugs me about his not being toilet trained. I have nightmares about being in the hospital and coming home to a child who has been spanked. My son will be two years old when the baby is born. Can she do permanent damage to him?

There are occasions when one has to explain that a grandparent cannot be allowed to take over unless he or she can follow directions from a parent. If there are real misgivings, one has to find alternatives: a husband taking some days off from his work; some other, less threatening relative or friend who could at least supervise. It is up to us grandparents to accept a parent's decision with grace and without feeling offended. And more often than not, it may be time to rethink our own behavior.

More of the same:

> How do I get my in-laws to respect my wishes regarding my children (ages one and four)? They allow my children to play in cars, give them candy, allow them to play outside alone, climb on kitchen counters, and don't insist on seat belts or car seats. I am concerned about nutrition and am very careful about what my children eat, but my in-laws give them whatever junk food they want. My older child told me that Grandma gives him the foods I don't allow and tells him that he'll get sick if he doesn't eat meat every day, for example. Do I find other baby-sitters? What shall I tell them?

Where health and safety are concerned, parents have every right to set firm limits. The children simply cannot visit grandparents if they are allowed to play alone in a car or on the street. The problem is that grandparents don't want to be the disciplinarians, they just want their grandchildren to have fun. Some grandparents confuse unconditional love with total permissiveness, and we need to understand that no matter how much grandparents want their grandchildren to love them, they must agree with their parents about the need for some controls while children are too young to control themselves.

Another letter describes a somewhat different dilemma:

> We live close to my in-laws, who seem obsessed with our toddler daughter. My mother-in-law tells strangers this is her daughter, not her granddaughter. She tells my daughter to call her "Mom," which is what my daughter calls me. She tells my child that I don't love her! My husband and father-in-law refuse to see this as a problem. When I try to discuss it, my mother-in-law heaps criticism on me.

Sometimes a family may have been denying a serious problem for years, refusing to deal with the fact that a family member may be emotionally disturbed. The mother may have to make it clear that she is the mother and her mother-in-law is the grandmother, and she is glad Grandma loves the child but that she cannot be allowed to confuse the roles. Until the child is a good deal older, it is not a good idea to permit baby-sitting unless one or the other parent is present. In this situation the mother must try to convince her father-in-law and husband that there is a serious problem that needs to be dealt with; the first step would be a thorough physical examination for Grandma, followed by consultation with a psychiatrist. Presenting herself as the mother of her granddaughter is serious. The problem may be menopausal; in any case, chances are she might be helped by the new armamentarium of psychotropic drugs.

On a similar theme:

> My problem is my mother-in-law, who has severe emotional problems due to being an abused child. When my first child was born,

she became very aggressive and bossy, trying to tell me how to raise her. At first she constantly threatened to kill me if I hurt her, but my daughter is now three, and Grandma has changed— now she wants me to spank her. I had another baby several months ago and, of course, the elder child is jealous and often difficult to handle. I know I must set limits, but I am against spanking. When my daughter accidently broke Grandma's teacup, Grandma got a switch, and before I knew what was happening, took down my child's pants and started whipping her. I stopped her, we left, I haven't seen her in weeks and she's very upset. I don't want to penalize her, but I have to protect my child. What can I do?

If any grandparent reading this book has ever "taken a switch" to a grandchild, it is time to seek counseling. Sometimes a grandparent may be reliving her own infancy and early child- hood through her grandchildren; obviously emotionally dis- turbed, she needs professional help. Parents must *never* allow a repetition of such behavior.

In a less serious vein, money and other gifts are often sources of contention between parents and grandparents. If we have a lot of money, our children may think we are stingy and selfish if we don't give the grandchildren elaborate presents. If we live on a tight budget, our children may resent the fact that we don't give enough. Some parents are annoyed if grandparents only buy luxuries for the grandchildren; some resent it if our presents are always practical and sensible. One mother told me, "My father buys the children ice cream every time he sees them because he's a diabetic and can't have any sweets!"

Often it's the grandchildren themselves who try to seduce us into buying silly, junky toys or duplicates of what they already have. I am putty in my granddaughter's hands in Toys R Us. But the older she gets, the more I try to encourage her to give real thought to her priorities. Sometimes grandchildren may have grandiose ideas of what we can give them because we love them so much. When Rhiannon asked us to buy her a horse, we got her a subscription to a horse magazine. But I must add that later, when she was older and we saw that the interest in horsemanship was not a temporary pleasure but a serious and intense commitment, we offered to lease a horse for her for one year by cutting the cost of a family midwinter vacation. When grandchildren are very young, I think it is legitimate to be a sucker to the degree that we can afford it. But by the time a grandchild is ten or eleven and able to control better the wish to have everything, we can help him or her to make choices, to ask for presents that will really be meaningful and satisfying for a long time. I suppose it comes down to at least understanding that a grandchild will want every teddy bear in sight at age four or five, but later insisting that twenty stuffed animals are sufficient, and other gifts might be more appropriate at seven, eight, or nine.

It's hard to avoid satisfying our own needs through our grandchildren. My daughter was never as interested in the theater as I was, so I had high hopes of having a grandchild who would want to be an actress! She, like her mother, is far more interested in horses. That's how it goes! If we happen to love sewing, knitting, fishing, football, gardening, bird watching, cooking, reading, but our grandchildren have other interests and get bored with ours, the only possible point of view we can take without damaging our relationship with them is that we can learn new things from what interests them.

It was a great disappointment to my father that none of his three grandchildren ever had the slightest interest in playing chess. He was a good sport about it, and enjoyed listening to them play the guitar and sing. Both my husband and I, who would never before have chosen to go to horse shows, have learned to enjoy sitting in the sun and watching the horses and the young riders, but our granddaughter knows that her joy in currying the horses and cleaning the stables leaves us cold. We know she will never enjoy some of the things we like to do. Let me rephrase that: We have no way of knowing what will interest her when she grows up, but whether she moves in our direction or in another, that's fine. What we like most is that everyone, including the grandchildren, should find their own song to sing, fully realizing their own interests and talents and becoming the most they can be in being themselves.

Gift-giving often expresses feelings that ought not be related to love. I now know that my mother unconsciously associated cakes, pies, candy, and expensive Christmas presents—too many of them—with showing how much she loved her grandchildren. Sometimes elaborate, expensive presents are the way in which we compete with the other set of grandparents. Or we give too much too soon because we feel guilty that in some way we deprived our children when they were young. When we buy fancy gifts, we are telling our grandchildren we only like store-bought presents. How can these compete with the things they make? If we know a good thing when we see it, we should much prefer the things our grandchildren make for us.

Our grandchildren find it very hard to believe that we *really* like the crooked clay candy dish, or the uneven potholders, the homemade cookies that weigh a pound and a half apiece, or the strictly modern art that needs an explanation. In this technological age of dolls that can carry on a conversation and computers for kids more complicated than Grandma's new microwave, how could they possibly think that the gifts they are able to make are likely to please us? A natural reaction, considering that we tend to give *them* all sorts of mechanical wonders—presents their parents can't afford, such as ten-speed bicycles and VCR's.

I *love* the things my granddaughter can make herself, and I know of only one way to convince her that the things we make have far more love in them than anything we can buy. That doesn't mean I might not behave like an old fool and spend far too much for a baby doll like the one I had when I was a child (now sixty-five dollars, it must have cost my parents all of two dollars). What it means is that even though I am really a lousy knitter and crocheter, I will make a hat and a scarf for that doll (I could *never* handle a sweater), and my granddaughter will know there was more love in that effort than in paying for the doll. She may not *use* the hat and scarf, and she may not *be crazy* about my handiwork, but she will be quite certain about the love.

If we want our grandchildren to feel happy and confident about the gifts they give us, we need to learn how to make something even if our sixty- or seventy-year-old skills don't even match theirs. The message is more important than the medium.

Another kind of loving is expressed in gifts of oneself. One grandmother found a note from her grandson that said, "Dear Grandma, my present is that on Christmas morning I will bring you breakfast in bed and be your slave all day." Grandma was truly thrilled, despite the fact that Danny's love was so great he included his pet frog on the breakfast tray along with the lumpy Wheatena and burned toast and chewable coffee. Her gift to him was, "If you are going to be my slave all day, I order you to accompany me to the Museum of Natural History!" A perfect exchange of gifts, speaking to a tender understanding of each other's needs. The very best of all possible gift-giving, without the stress of shopping or the danger of bankruptcy.*

Money certainly enters into our relationships with our adult children. One young woman told me how difficult it was to have a job with an infant at home. Day care and baby-sitters

---

*There is an excellent book to help you choose gifts for children: *Buy Me! Buy Me!: A Bank Street Guide for Choosing Toys for Children* by Joanne Oppenheim and published by Pantheon.

could easily absorb most of her earnings. Then she said, "I called my mother and asked her to send me a thousand dollars. I shouldn't have had to ask; she and my father have plenty of money. I can't understand when they don't just give it to us without being asked."

I didn't say anything—except that I was sorry for her financial stress. But later, because I am the age of her parents, I did a double take: Why should she *expect* them to give her money? Whatever they have, they earned. They are now retired and want to enjoy the fruits of their labor. They don't *owe* her anything.

Whenever a young adult feels "they owe me," I wonder about what we are dealing with; it's probably old business. Unless there is a genuine financial crisis, the request, the expectation may be a feeling that parents were neglectful and rejecting when he or she was a child. There was always the hope that by being "good" one could get more attention and affection. Unconsciously some adult children feel that having tried to measure up in every way, they should have received more rewards.

None of us ever wants to hear our progeny tell us we "owe" them. At first glance it is infuriating, but the attitude needs to be examined. Had we expected too much? Had we ever indicated that love was tied to performance? Behind the "you owe me" is the statement, "You never really were satisfied with me, and nothing I've done has changed that."

It's not easy for any of us to give a lot of financial help when we have our own terrors of financial dependency. But thousands of grandparents who find their children and grandchildren in far worse financial straits than when *they* were young—however reluctantly and fearfully (because of concern for their own futures)—don't have to be asked to help when the need is legitimate and the gift is not going to represent a serious or overwhelming sacrifice.

You may have noticed that I mention Grandma more often than Grandpa on the issue of childraising rights and the responsibilities. In the past, most women played a far more central role in raising children. Few men feel guilty if their sons and daughters have new and different approaches to parenthood. Perhaps in future generations, now that Father takes a more active part in childraising, they, too, may feel threatened or frustrated by the way their grandchildren are being raised. At the present time, it is mostly grandmothers who get agitated, and mostly grandfathers who tell their wives to cool it. But this is a generality that misses the exceptions. I know one grandfather whose tone of voice with his grandchildren sounds like a father more than a grandfather. When he reprimands one of his grandsons, he is as forceful as he ever was as a parent. I marvel at how his son and daughter-in-law put up with it! When he visits, his opening greeting is likely to be, "Okay, boys, let me see your math papers!" Some grandfathers tend to be shy with babies; some fight off grandmothers to hold the baby. Some grandfathers keep their distance until a grandchild is old enough to play baseball or go fishing. Some grandfathers may not relate too well in making normal, everyday conversation with grandchildren but tell wonderful stories.

Of course, there are as many different kinds of grandfathers as there are people. But my general impression is that, as a group, they are somewhat more detached than grandmothers.

This may well be because if you are old enough to be a grandfather you were probably raised not to express your emotions too readily. Fortunately, younger generations of boys are hopefully being raised to believe that men are allowed to cry, that men and women can share their feelings, and that fathers can be as involved in child care as much as mothers. The next generation of grandfathers will probably be more open and communicate more fully with their grandchildren.

But for our generation, I think grandmothers need to be more encouraging, more willing to share this new role. Too often Grandma enjoys being the one a baby turns to more easily, and she doesn't encourage Grandpa to ask for equal time. I remember feeling uncomfortable when my infant granddaughter seemed glad to see me and started to cry the minute Grandpa walked into the room. He was confused and hurt. Before we settled too easily into a theory of rejection, we finally figured out it was the heavy, dark frames on his glasses. I could have been a selfish pig about it, but I was very relieved when we could both have a relationship with this precious child.

With many exceptions, of course, grandparents will each have a very different relationship with grandchildren, and that's just fine. Children need to be exposed to all kinds of differences. Whatever liberated women may say, I have never met an adorable little girl grandchild who didn't flirt with Grandpa. There may be some, but I have never encountered any. And because of the interests of most grandfathers, little boys are more inclined to want to build with blocks, play with a fire engine, or play ball with grandfathers. I am personally inclined to believe quite firmly in natural, inherent differences—it may be training, but I don't buy it! Few boys want to play "house" with Grandpa. Sometimes it may appear to others that grandfathers aren't as close to their grandchildren, and it is true that most men— fathers and grandfathers—are inclined to react differently to different ages and stages of children, perhaps responding more as the children get older. Sometimes a deep relationship just isn't as visible. Grandmas are more prone to hug and kiss and coo. But children may be just as aware of the man in the background who merely smiles.

Grandma may have to learn to allow Grandpa to make his own overtures in his own way and trust children to figure him out. I think we have a tendency to interfere too much. Grandma says, "Fred, why don't you give Seth a hug?" while Grandpa and Seth both look embarrassed and uncomfortable. Left to doing what comes naturally, Seth and Grandpa will come to their own distinct and unique relationship, and the last thing they need is an interfering Grandma.

It is not uncommon for grandparents to differ sharply on issues such as discipline, just as parents do. Grandpa, raised by a stern, autocratic father, may think a good spanking is occasionally called for; Grandma, who went to a lot of parent education classes while raising their children, fought him hard, and there may still be a residue of their differences. Grandpa may feel his wife interfered too much when they were raising their children, but now, as a grandfather, he can express himself more freely. The best cure for this is to accept the fact that discipline is not the function of the grandparents. It is when we are alone with grandchildren—when they visit they know things will be different from at home. We have to interfere when a grandchild suddenly decides to cross a street alone, or throw mud at another kid in the sandbox, or won't hold our hand at a crowded amusement park or fair. Of course, we have to make such decisions, but a basic principle is to let parents raise their own children and for us to love and have fun with them.

I remember my mother telling my father to play with my daughter when we visited their summer home. She would say, "Max, why don't you take Wendy for a walk, or pick some apples, or let her help you make that rock garden?" I wished she would shut up and let Wendy and my father find their own ways of relating, which they did.

One of the most useful things about having parents and grandparents, aunts and uncles, family friends, and teachers is that this is how children learn that each person is different and we need to relate to each other in unique styles. One of the best things about grandfathers is that they are not grandmothers! I have never yet met a grandfather who got so distraught when grandchildren went through the adolescent (temporary) need to separate from grandparents. They either take it in stride or never even notice it and think their wives are imagining the whole thing.

I have always encouraged parents to tell their children about their own childhood. It helps the children understand why they behave so differently. Larry's mother made a big fuss about table manners, so he was pretty rigid about that. When Wendy kicked the table legs, or mashed up her food, or was too squirmy, he was wont to shout, "CIVILIZE UP!" I would comfort Wendy in the kitchen and say he was fussy because of his childhood. On Saturday mornings when I became a screaming maniac about Wendy cleaning up her room (my mother had done the same thing to me), Larry would say, "Come on, Wendy. Let's go to the playground until your mother calms down." I was grateful. I had sworn as a child I'd never behave the way my mother had, but I seemed unable to control my behavior. We can help grandchildren understand their parents.

Grandparents can tell a lot about their own childhood and why they turned out to be so different. They also can explain why parents are different. They can tell about another time, another world. The best history lessons are rarely taught in school, where too often memorized dates are more important than the culture, the human relations, of a particular period. What grandparents tell about the events of their own early lives can give a new perspective to children about how times change, how new inventions influence the climate of life. The thing is, grandmothers should let grandfathers tell their stories in their own way in their own time.

I had never thought very much about reluctant grandparents until I began to get letters from unhappy parents who felt rejected because their parents didn't seem to want to be involved with the grandchildren. A typical letter:

> I have three daughters, five, three, and one. My husband helps me a lot, we have a good sitter, but my mother lives fifteen minutes away, and I hesitate to call her to baby-sit because 90 percent of the time she either says no, or if she comes, she acts as if it is a hardship. All my children behave very well. My mother says I should hire a maid (which I can't afford) and that she wants to be a grandma, not a sitter. It bothers me that my children see so little of their grandmother. My father died two years ago. I have no relatives nearby.

It is always better if a grandparent can explain his or her behavior. Often grandparents feel they have raised a family and that they are finished with childraising. Or they get tired more easily than ever before. To care for three children under age six is no laughing matter for even relatively young grandparents. It helps if adult child and parent can talk about these kinds of issues—express feelings of rejections and resentment on one side, and feelings of being expected to do too much on the other side. My guess in relation to this particular letter was that possibly Grandma was still in a state of mourning, unable to bear the thought that she couldn't share her grandchildren with her husband, and was too depressed to have much energy. What a difference it could make if this daughter could have said, "I know you still grieve for Daddy. I wish I could help you. Could you help me pay for a sitter once in a while? Then I'd be home when you come to see the children, and we could even have dates and go out to a movie and dinner, because I know you're lonely and depressed." Being understood, talking about feelings, could help this grandmother participate more fully in her grandchildren's lives.

Sometimes jealousy or rivalry with brothers and sisters cause parents to feel that their children are being rejected by grand-parents. Another letter:

> I have a problem with my parents and brothers. I am married and have two young children. My parents never come to see us but expect us to travel to see them. My brothers never even acknowledged the births of our children.

It doesn't take Sherlock Holmes to figure out that there is some old unfinished business here! Since I feel so strongly that children need grandparents, I think there are times when adult children need to try to confront their parents, in this case to try to discuss (calmly and quietly, if possible!) feelings that parents preferred other siblings and that this was and remains extremely painful. My hope would be that grandparents will be mature enough to try to listen and learn.

Parents are often inclined to expect their parents to be available at a moment's notice for baby-sitting, and will love it. Many times this is not true. But creative ingenuity is the name of the game. When her son called to say he needed to bring his three young children to Grandma's house because his wife had to go to the hospital, a Grandma said, "Fine, of course," and as soon as she hung up the phone she called a nanny agency and hired a full-time baby-sitter! She said, "I love the children, they're very cute, and I played with them ten minutes here, ten minutes there—and it worked out just fine!"

Often a reluctance, a disinterest in participating actively as a grandparent depends on the age of the child as well as the age of the grandparent. A grandmother will say, "My daughter has to understand I changed my last diaper when she learned to go to the potty!" Or a grandfather will say, "I never knew how to talk to children, even my own, until they got interested in baseball." No one has any choice about what age we prefer when we are parents; grandparents often feel that they have that choice. Another grandparent says, "My daughter doesn't understand how exhausted I get even baby-sitting for an hour or two."

We lose too much if we are too self-absorbed, tired, unwilling to make some effort. Grandchildren lose a vital relationship, but perhaps we lose even more: a sense of connectedness to the future, a sense of immortality through our grandchildren.

Part of the answer may be to try to relate to grandchildren in one's own idiosyncratic way. There are no laws about what makes a good or a bad grandparent. The soup-giver, the always-ready caretaker may be one nice kind of grandparent to have. A grandfather who appears twice a year and tells funny jokes or tall tales may mean as much or more to his grandchildren than the grandfather who is nervous and anxious and keeps saying, "Don't do this." Grandparents who travel and send letters and picture postcards may be giving their own grandchildren a healthy desire for adventure in their own lives, while the grandparents who are always there for Thanksgiving dinner may be providing a feeling of security and stability.

When we "do our own thing" we can bring more zest and pleasure to being grandparents, but we need to remember we are the only maternal or paternal grandparents these grand-children will ever have, and if we are reasonably mature and compassionate we may need to make a special effort to find some relatively comfortable way to play a part in their lives. At the same time, we may need to make an effort to help our children understand our needs and feelings.

Many of my grandparent friends today have full-time or part-time jobs. Or, if they and their husbands have retired, it is almost always after many years of hard work, and they are looking forward to a time when they can have the freedom for travel, for developing new hobbies, for having new adventures. They are in better health than their grandparents were. On the other hand, some of them are just plain *tired*, and the playfulness of children wears them out. I saw a woman in a supermarket the other day; I was afraid she was going to have a heart attack or a stroke as she tried to shop with two wild kids. I had the feeling that they had been visiting for much too long.

My granddaughter is beautiful, lovable, and interesting, but playing Monopoly at 5:00 A.M. almost killed me. I have a "god-child" who is absolutely adorable; I love him dearly. I don't want to change diapers at age seventy-one, and I don't want to run after him to keep him from electrocuting himself—he's mad for wires and sockets right now. I adore watching toddlers—my favorite age range is two to four—but watching is the limit of my strength. It makes me sad; I would love to be thirty-five again. I think that when our children see us failing as grandparents it is partly because they cannot bear the idea that we are getting old.

I have a young friend with a new baby; the friend is furious (but is really feeling rejected and hurt) because her wealthy parents haven't invited her to visit them at their condo in Hawaii. Her parents go there for three or four months every winter. They are in their late sixties.

I understand her hurt feelings, but I am also in sympathy with her parents. There comes a time when parenting and grandparenting are *enough already*! Given the chance to rekindle the romance in an old marriage, soak one's old bones in sunshine, and not have to plan a damn thing all day is part of what growing older should be all about. It doesn't mean we don't love our families, just that we have given all we've got and it is time for a sabbatical. When grandparents may seem disinterested, it may be because their children expect too much.

I received this letter from a forty-two-year-old mother:

> My parents live in Florida, and while they are devoted to each other, they are woefully out of touch with my children, although

I am a good daughter to them. They did not attend my son's bar mitzvah, and they send ten-dollar Chanukah presents when they could easily afford F.A.O. Schwarz! My husband's parents are worse: They live twenty minutes away and you have to beg them to come to some important event for the children. The children never had overnight visits, never were taken to Disneyland or anywhere else. On the rare occasions when we get together, none of the grandparents spends time talking to the children!

I remember how shocked I was with the way my mother-in-law behaved with my child. She never invited her to visit at any time during my daughter's childhood—not once; the only personal thing I can remember is that once, when we visited, she set Wendy's hair. I thought that was remarkable! I have no idea what her behavior meant. Now I wish I had asked her. Could we have made her feel that any overtures were unwelcome? Was she "burned out" from raising three children as a widow?

Most grandparents are overjoyed to have grandchildren. Many grandparents have greatly missed having little kids around and revel in having new playmates. Most grandparents are like me, I think, full of love but easily tired! However, parents must face the fact that there can be a number of reasons why some grandparents aren't cut out to play an active role very well.

One reason is simply burnout related to childraising and needing to be alone together. Adult children should be glad when parents are still that crazy about each other. Other people see grandchildren as clear indications that they are getting old, and this is unendurable—they prefer to deny the passage of time. Some people had a very hard time raising children in the first place and are frankly glad to be free at last.

The worst thing parents can do is make the grandchildren feel that this is somehow their fault; they should be cuter or more polite or better behaved. Children need the truth; they sense it whether you say anything or not. Much better to say some people don't like getting older and that having grandchildren reminds them of it, and some people are tired and children wear them out, and some people just aren't too wonderful with their own or anyone else's children. A mother said, "I never felt my mother really liked me, but I was sure she would melt when she saw my adorable baby." Not necessarily. People who weren't crazy about being parents aren't too likely to have a major personality change as grandparents. Resentment and anger by adult children and guilt and defensiveness by grandparents are no service to grandchildren.

If we are decent and civilized and understand the needs, the vulnerability, of young children, it seems to me we have to make an effort to meet the needs of our grandchildren at least some of the time, limiting ourselves to what we can do and not feeling guilty about what we can't do.

I think it's just fine to insist on your right to freedom and quiet and rest. But there are other things to consider. Nobody loses so much by no contact with young people than older people. The child inside each of us dries up and dies. And whatever our age, maturity means making some demands on ourselves. In addition, these children *are* our immortality, and one of these days we may regret it if they hardly remember us at all.

I believe grandchildren need us; that our children are right when they say we should come to graduations and piano recitals; that we should visit at least once or twice a year; that we should call and write and remember birthdays. It's also good for us. But some of us may need to remind our children that overinvolvement can be a nuisance.

The counterpoint to reluctant grandparents is my friend who has three grown sons. She tells me, "You better believe I'm cultivating the girlfriend and the two wives! I'm so adorable and lovable—I wait on them hand and foot. This is my insurance policy that they will let me hang out with my grandchildren as much as I want!" I imagine it's possible that one or more of these daughters-in-law will wish for a little less overwhelming devotion!

The nice thing about being a grandparent is *not* having to act like a parent. A friend of mine told me, "My grandson was playing in the backyard, all by himself. I was watching him from the kitchen window, and for a few minutes I couldn't figure out what he was doing—he seemed to be grabbing at the air. I went outside to ask him—he was five years old at the time. He told me he was 'catching sunbeams'! What a poetic, creative child!" I asked her if she had ever watched her children with the same intensity when they were playing alone, and she said, "Who had the time?" As grandparents not responsible for the daily lives of children, we have the time to notice, time to join in play and fantasy. We can be fellow poets. Few other adults have time for quiet reflection, repose, imaginative play with young children.

One of the best resources we can be in the lives of grandchildren is to serve as role models. Are we active in politics? Do we take our citizenship seriously? Are we trying to keep ourselves in shape? Do we help other people? Are we good to our friends? Do we give ourselves time to be alone, or to take an art class, or to go back to college for some courses that interest us? The reason Auntie Mame was so good for her nephew is that she lived such a full and satisfying life, always aware that "life is a banquet" and she was going to enjoy every bit of it.

We can be role models about areas that may not be significant to young children directly but that can teach them about patience and courage when we are ill, or handicapped by problems of aging. Our attitudes toward retirement, marriage, recreation, even our feelings about death and dying may make much more of an impression than we realize. I have very clear memories about my grandmother, even when she didn't know what she was talking about but was telling me what she thought was right. Every time I see leaves on trees blowing in the wind with the backs of the leaves showing, I remember my grandmother telling me that meant it might rain. It doesn't work. She also said if I burned my tongue, I should take some more of whatever was too hot—heat would cure heat. She also said never put water on a burn, only butter. I never follow her directions now; I do my own thing, but I have the loving memory, because the essential ingredient of our relationship was that she loved me.

I asked a five-year-old what she thought grandparents should do, and before she could answer, her mother said, with deep feeling, "Be good to the mother of the grandchildren!" One day I met a grandmother I knew, in the library. Her daughter and grandchildren were our neighbors. I had just heard that one of the children had had a fight with another child in the playground. She had been struck near her eye and had to be taken to the doctor. I told the grandmother her grandchild was recovering nicely but her daughter was beside herself with terror over what almost had happened. Grandma said, "My God! I've been out all day—I didn't know—I'll go right over." I suggested her daughter needed more motherly comforting than her granddaughter. She paid no attention. My neighbor said, "My mother ran into the apartment, went straight to Cathy, interrupting her play when she had already recovered from the trauma, and paid no attention to me. How I wished she had put her arms about me and said, 'You poor child' and let me have a good cry on her shoulder!" Sometimes the best way we can help our grandchildren is to continue to nurture and support their parents. A grandfather reminisced about a time when his son-in-law failed the state bar exams for the second time. "He was wrecked," he said, "the children were scared to death, he was so depressed and angry, yelling at them to be quiet, to leave him alone. I told him he and I were going on a fishing boat for the day. I told him he was doing the best he could, that I was proud of him for trying so hard, that if needed, we could help a bit until he passed the tests. When we got back to his house that night, he hugged the children."

Helping our own children is often the best way to help the grandchildren. Giving parents a weekend away from the kids, helping to ease a depression over a lost job, comforting them when a child is seriously ill, supporting them when they make a mistake—buying the wrong car, choosing a house too far from other children, yelling too much and then feeling guilty. It helps parents to feel better if we remind them of *our* failures with *them*! And how they turned out just fine despite our imperfections. At age fifty, when my mother died, I had a piercing sensation of pain because she could never hug me, I could never tell her my troubles. We never get over needing nurturing parents. The more we comfort our own adult children, the more they can comfort our grandchildren.

4

Ages and Stages in Child Development

IT IS STRANGE but true that although we may have learned all sorts of important facts while raising our own children, when we become grandparents we still tend to forget a whole lot of things we knew.

A neighbor told me, "When Trudy bit me, I was furious! Also very hurt. I was trying to put her down for her nap and she was mad at me. My first thought was, Who needs a nasty, mean grandchild? It took me a few minutes to remember she was two years old and her father had done the same thing when he was two."

It is so easy for us to misinterpret behavior if we don't know what is appropriate at a given age. One grandmother asked me, "Is it possible for a child to pick up negative feelings from a parent and act on them accordingly? I have a one-year-old grandchild who cries and reaches for her mother or father when I'm around. If I talk to her she turns her back and walks away." This grandmother is assuming one or both parents don't like her. The simplest and most certainly truer conclusion is that one-year-olds have a very hard time with anyone who comes between them and their parents. It is a normal developmental sequence to discover that parents can appear and disappear, and this is a painful new awareness. Grandma, if she will keep her distance, smiling lovingly, for a very short time, will be back in her granddaughter's good graces as the strong dependency on the two most important people in the world begins to lessen somewhat.

We tend to lose our perspective with grandchildren. We probably expected it to be hard to raise our children—but *grandchildren* were supposed to be perfect and love us all the time! Here were these adorable creatures we loved and spoiled and for whom we would do anything to make them happy—and then they can turn on us in a flash.

It seems to me to be a good idea to provide a little refresher about the nature of childhood; it may be that as grandparents we're supposed to have all the fun and none of the work, but children don't always understand that distinction. A friend of mine who is a therapist working with adolescents—and who is a very good one, too—was devastated when her ten-year-old granddaughter didn't want her to be at her birthday party. I had to remind her about "peer pressure" and how self-conscious kids are about being popular, being "cool." Grandmothers are not supposed to hang around making kids feel like babies. My friend looked startled and laughed. "If I'd been seeing her in my office, I would have understood how she felt, but we've had such a love affair all along, I forgot she would grow up!"

There are patterns of growth and behavior that are common to most children sooner or later at their own pace, and as grandparents we may need to remember what we once knew. And then there are some grandparents who had little opportunity to be exposed to much in the way of theories of child psychology while they were busy practicing being parents. For both young or older grandparents, there are more new ideas about child nature all the time. And we can be beneficiaries of these new ideas, or old ones we have forgotten.

There are many books on child development,* and it's not a bad idea for grandparents to reread Dr. Spock as well as some more recent authors. All I want to do here is mention a few highlights of normal feelings and behavior of each developmental stage to remind us of those that seem most useful.

INFANCY

I met a friend for lunch who had recently become a grandmother. She seemed very distraught; she said, "Oh, I'm so worried about Annie. She looks terrible, she's thin as a rail, she isn't getting enough sleep." The problem was that Grandma's two-month-old granddaughter was crying on and off all night. With a husband who had to travel during the week, there was no one to give Annie any relief. "Annie runs in to Sharon the minute she starts crying. I think she should just let her cry; sooner or later she would wear herself out."

I told Grandma that the best way she could help would be to baby-sit for a few hours a week and let Annie take some naps during the day but that her "solution" to the problem seemed wrong to me.

Infants are not deliberately trying to drive their parents to an early grave! It is *not* a power struggle. Babies have no notion of time or space. Alone in a room, they have no way of figuring out if anyone will ever come back; they have no idea of spatial

*My own being *When Your Child Drives You Crazy* and *In Search of Myself and Other Children*, both paperbacks published by St. Martin's Press.

relations, no way to figure out that there are rooms outside their own, no idea where another person might be. All a baby can feel is some disorganized, vague sense of terror: Will anyone harm me? Is there anyone else in the world? When infants cry, they need to be comforted. If from time to time one takes the baby into one's own bed for a while, this will not be habit-forming; babies have never heard of habits or of being spoiled— they just feel their needs. Or if parents want to keep a baby in the child's own bed, they will have to come into the room and sit with the baby in a rocking chair and do whatever else needs to be done to give comfort. The loss of sleep does need to be made up at least in part by husbands and wives taking turns, by having a baby-sitter during the day so a parent can sleep for a few hours. If a mother has to return to work, then she and her husband should bring in a cooked supper and even take a nap before bedtime. We must find ways to make arrangements when we believe that infants need to be comforted, not left alone to cry. It also helps to understand that it is a temporary problem.

Within a few months at most, babies begin to see the outside world more clearly; they recognize other rooms and people in them; they begin to understand that they are never totally alone; if they cry because they are hungry or wet, they begin to per-ceive that someone will come, so that once their needs are met, they can go back to sleep.

It is a mistake ever to think that infants are consciously trying to control the universe! What can they possibly know about anyone else's needs? I assured Grandma that Annie's tour of constant duty would end just as soon as her baby's brain was able to comprehend that comfort is always available. Then the sense of terror and loneliness gradually decreases. Hopefully grandparents, out of love for their adult children, will not sug-gest abandoning grandchildren by letting them "cry it out."

PRESCHOOL YEARS

If I had my way, nursery school teachers would be paid much more than college professors. These years, from about two to five, are, in my opinion, the most important years in a child's growth. More important learning takes place than ever again. Language has a lot to do with it. Once a human being can have thoughts that may or may not be put into action, fundamental religious, ethical, and psychological challenges are in motion.

Grandpa, watching his son bathe the newborn baby, is shocked when a four-year-old brother tries to push the baby's head under the water, saying, "I can teach Joel to swim." Daddy says, "I guess you would like to drown Joel because he takes up so much time, but I can't let you hurt him." Grandpa later says to his son, "Why in the world did you bring up such a terrible thought? That was ridiculous!" It was not; Grandpa should be proud of a son who has such insight! Actually, the older brother needed to be reassured that "bad thoughts" couldn't make bad things happen. This is the stage of the angel and the devil: How do I figure out the loving and the hating parts of myself? How do I keep some of my thoughts under control?

Once, when my four-year-old daughter was mad at me, she yelled, "Go away and never come back!" And then she looked terrified and said, "But don't you dare go downstairs!" Preschool children have to learn the most fundamental rules of psychology and human relationships, and what they learn will be with them all their lives. The task is to understand that everybody has angry, jealous, hateful feelings some of the time and loving, happy, friendly feelings as well. It's a terribly difficult thing to figure out. Children have their own ways of dealing with the problem. One way is to have an imaginary playmate; it's the imaginary pet rabbit who gets into trouble, or it's an imaginary naughty boy named Fred. By turning over one's "bad side" to another creature, one can feel safe about being good. Another solution is to become very afraid of horses or cats or vacuum cleaners or thunder that makes a loud noise. Fears of the less wonderful side of being human are externalized to animals and inanimate objects. An angelic little girl in a nursery school where I was observing was wearing a lovely dress with a taffeta slip and shiny Mary Janes, looking positively delectable. She ran up to the teacher and said, "I am a bad tiger and I'm going to scratch your eyes out and eat you!" The teacher sat Penny on her lap and calmly said, "Sometimes you are a pretty, friendly little girl, and sometime you feel like an angry tiger." The teacher got an A+ from me! What she was doing was helping Penny accept the human equation—the devil and the angel in all of us. If Penny had begun to act out being a tiger, the teacher would have said (and gotten another A+!), "It is okay to feel angry sometimes, but I won't let you hurt me or anyone else." Imagine: Between two and five years a child has to learn the difference between having a normal feeling and controlling behavior. During this period, children want to know that if they have impulses they can't yet control, adults will provide the controls.

When a grandchild says, "Grandma, I love you!" it is natural to feel delighted and loving. When a grandchild says, "You're a dope!" it is not helpful to respond, "That's a naughty, rude thing to say." What provides a better learning sequence would be to say, "Maybe you are feeling angry at me and you can tell me, but calling me 'a dope' hurts my feelings." That sets limits on behavior without cutting off feelings.

Language, as it communicates thoughts and feelings, seems so wonderful. When Donald tells us, "I can spell 'cat' and 'hat' and 'bat' and 'sat,' " we thank Dr. Seuss and applaud such a smart four-year-old. And when Amy says, "Grandma, I like the color of your hair—you look younger than my other grandma," language seems positively lovely. However, may I remind you that language is power to a three- or four-year-old. Learning to say "no" was the Declaration of Independence—they have been dizzy with power ever since. They have discovered that language is a wonderful way of getting both positive and negative attention, and some words learned in nursery school can make grandparents get red in the face and angry and unhappy.

This seems absolutely fascinating, and for a year or two, the "bad words" are very exciting. If adults make a big fuss over "doo-doo" and "pee-pee" and "damn" and "stupid," the words will last longer and get worse. Laughter and joining in by making up silly sounds ourselves is more fun and tends to make the period of shock language shorter. Don't get excited! It is certainly appropriate to say, "Some grown-ups will feel unfriendly if you use those words in front of them. Some of them bother me, too. The best place to say them as much as you want to would be in your room." Hopefully, you have noticed, I didn't suggest saying the words are "bad" or the children "naughty"!

Frustration is often clear in the behavior of preschool-age children. Temper tantrums are the most obvious, with biting, hitting, and kicking also normal behavior. Adults have to acknowledge what the child is feeling but stop unacceptable behavior. "I know how angry you are because you're not big enough to go on your sister's bicycle," or "It's scary to be so angry that you can't stop yourself from kicking, but I can't let you do that because it hurts," or during a tantrum, "When you're feeling better we can talk about what upsets you so much; meanwhile, I guess you need a little time to be by yourself."

Beyond the issue of accepting feelings but controlling behavior lies the most important message we can give a young child: He or she is not "bad" but only "young." I know of nothing that leaves more psychic scars than to think of oneself as bad, unlovable, unworthy. Those of us who may suffer as adults because we are trying too hard to be "good" to everyone but ourselves, often at the price of low self-esteem, surely don't want this to be a legacy to our grandchildren!

SCHOOL AGE

Gradually, between five and seven years, grandchildren are very likely to become much more interested in other children than in continuing a love affair with grandparents. This is entirely appropriate; it is the beginning of a long process of moving away from being a dependent child and joining one's own generation.

But while they may not want to sit on our laps, and hugging and kissing become embarrassing, there is one aspect of growth in which we can still play a major part: School-age children are curious, hungry to learn, to have new adventures. They still like to be read to; they love places like the Museum of Natural History. I still remember our granddaughter's breathless excitement at her first view of a dinosaur skeleton, her joyous wonder at the zoo, watching a baby gorilla climb onto its mother's back and cling so tight it didn't fall off no matter how the mother moved around.

Trips are something special that grandparents can offer; Disneyland, if we can endure it; postcards from foreign places; a gift of an arrowhead from a trip out West when the third grade studies Native Americans. The elementary school years have to do with new kinds of fears: Will other children like me? Will teachers think I'm smart? Am I dumb if I have trouble reading or doing addition and subtraction? Will other kids be mad at me if I'm better than anybody in the class at multiplication? What if other children tease me? What if I'm the last one chosen for the soccer team?

These are major concerns, and in attempting to deal with

them, children tend to make an assumption that the safest course is to be exactly like "everyone" else.

Grandma has a fit when eight-year-old Jacob insists on letting his hair grow in the back in a small ponytail. She thinks he looks ridiculous. Maybe—but Grandma needs to let Jacob know she respects his need to follow the fashion at this time in his life and that he will grow and change.

These are the years that have to do with power and skills. It's a good time for a hands-off policy. A grandfather says, "My son and daughter-in-law told me I could be *interested* in Alexander's grades but never *critical*. I'm trying hard to walk this tightrope! I can take him swimming and we can enjoy the water, but I have to remember swimming *lessons* are for the YMCA counselor, not me."

The five-to-twelve crowd wants grandparents to be proud of all their achievements—come to plays and sports events, enjoy all successes, but never show disappointment or disapproval over failures. Parents and teachers can deal with that. Sympathy is okay but must not be excessive—no tears, please. One ten-year-old summed up what should be appropriate behavior for grandparents. She said, "If you feel too sorry for me because I have a mean teacher, that doesn't help me. Mommy will go to talk to the principal. I like it when we do interesting things together, but not all the time. Grandparents can get boring." I couldn't have agreed more with my granddaughter, Rhiannon. (Adolescence will be dealt with in the next chapter.)

IN GENERAL

While it is thoroughly admirable to want to be as knowledgeable as possible about normal child development, we have to be careful that we behave in ways that support the parents of our grandchildren.

Unfortunately, there are times when we say things impulsively, without thinking. One father told me that he and his wife and two children had gone to visit a toy factory in Maine. Daddy's mother later asked her daughter-in-law, "Did you buy some new stuffed animals?" Meg said no, the children's room was swamped with too many toys already. Grandma turned to the grandchildren and said, "That's terrible! Your parents are mean to you! Next year I'll go with you and buy you some new toys." This is not only undermining parental controls but also setting up a competition between parents and grandparents.

A grandfather was very worried because he could tell his daughter was dying to have a third child although she and her husband couldn't manage financially even with two children. In the course of discussing this matter and without thinking, he shouted, "DON'T EVEN *THINK* ABOUT HAVING ANY MORE KIDS!" He knew immediately he had overstepped the line. It was one thing to have discussed the pros and cons calmly, but we must constantly remind ourselves of the limits of our authority. Competing with parents is a form of interference. Grandpa says, "I can teach you the multiplication tables *much* better than your daddy can." Or Grandma says, "I'll take you shopping for your school clothes—your mother has terrible taste in clothes."

One grandmother told me this story: Her five-year-old grandson, with whom she had a very close relationship, called her on the telephone. He said, "Grandma, I need your help. Mommy won't let me watch any television in the daytime, and even though it's summertime I only can watch a half hour before supper. I think she's very mean. Will you tell her?" Grandma responded, "Well, Ted, I can see your mom's point of view. Most days you can go swimming, and play in the sandbox, and see your little friends, and go on the swings and the slides in the playground, and when it rains you have clay and paints and maybe Mom can let you cook with her. I'll tell you what: Why don't you draw some pictures to go with the story I told you last week? We could make it into a book!"

Grandma didn't interfere with her daughter-in-law's rules. What she did was distract and offer alternatives.

There are times when grandparents think a grandchild is a genius; sometimes they are right. There are times when they reel with joy at burgeoning signs of special talents; sometimes they are right. There are times when grandparents feel that grandchildren are being pushed too hard to excel in school, or spoiled, or allowed to "get away with murder," or are "emotionally disturbed and need expert help." Any of these observations may be true; the important thing is that they may be false. One of the most difficult things we have to learn is to mind our own business and at the same time offer our opinions if asked to do so, but never suggest we are sure of any answers.

Sometimes our children ask for our views. They may be worried or confused by a child's behavior. If we think we can be helpful, that's fine as long as we are aware of some pitfalls.

I knew a young couple who had a little girl whom they felt was hyperactive. There were no living grandparents, so Larry and I attempted to play that role. When I saw the child at one and a half, I made nothing of their fears. I said that her short attention span was perfectly normal for her age and personality and that they should stop worrying—they were being overanxious. Boy, was I wrong! By three, Barbara was clearly an autistic child. Instead of shutting off the observations and concerns, I should have said, "If you're really worried, I can find out where you can get expert advice."

In another case, a grandmother told me, "Debbie is the most stubborn child I have ever seen. You just can't change her mind whatever you say or do. I told my son he and my daughter-in-law should take her to see a psychiatrist." Grandma was so absolutely convinced she was right that Liz's parents became equally upset. After a few visits the therapist told them, "Tell Grandma to relax and mind her own business! This is one great kid. She's so bright and so talented that all you have to do is say, 'Go, girl, go!' "

We ought not to be alarmist or to reassure too easily and quickly. What we can do is be good listeners and help parents turn to others for professional evaluations. We are too close, care too much, even if we have the training.

If our grandchildren are lucky, they have four grandparents to love them unconditionally. It is delightful if all four (and these days there can even be a sprinkling of great-grandparents) are fond of each other. Whether they are or not, young children ought not be made confused or anxious by competition or rivalry among people they love. We need to be aware that trying to outdo each other in the gift-giving department or saying anything derogatory about "the other" grandparents is not helpful. Children will begin to understand the nuances of these relationships quickly enough as they become older and better able to understand and handle any necessary realities. At age eleven, Liz told her grandmother, "I used to wonder why you never see my other nana and poppa. But I guess you were too angry at them when Daddy went to live with Susan and left me and Mom." At three, when it happened, Liz was far too young and in too much pain herself to be required to deal with the animosity among her grandparents.

If other grandparents provide luxuries, shower the children with too many toys, or are overly permissive, we can refuse to go to war. If other grandparents are indifferent or neglectful, we need to be mature enough to offer acceptable explanations ("too tired, too sick, too many worries") even if our opinion is quite different. It's definitely the wrong time of life for any such confrontations.

We have one great advantage over parents: We may not be able to remember why we are walking from one room to another, or where we left our glasses or wallet—and we are rapidly forgetting the names of our nearest and dearest, but we *are* remembering more and more about our own childhood! It seems to be a "normal developmental sequence" in the process of aging.

The older I get, the more I remember my childhood, from age two or three. Even more than events, I remember feelings more and more vividly. This is the most valuable asset one can bring to childraising. If you remember your own early feelings, you are far better able to understand children and grandchildren. You can remember feeling terribly afraid to go in the water; you can remember hating certain foods; you can remember a feeling of desolation, terror, the first day in a new school.

When I meet and talk with young parents I exhort them to *try to remember*. But this doesn't come naturally for most of them. They are caught in the busyness of daily life, in the stresses of work and marriage and parenthood. It is quite natural to have forgotten—repressed—a great many memories that start to reappear to consciousness as we get older.

One of the ways in which we can play a vital part in the lives of our grandchildren without interfering with parental prerogatives is to let them know we understand what they may be going through. Rhiannon often looks quite startled if I comment casually, "I remember that when I was your age make-believe seemed so real, I could hardly tell which was which." Or Larry says, "I can think of twenty times when I felt like running away, but knew I had no place to go." Being able to acknowledge, share a feeling, is a wonderful way to offer our companionship.

It is a delight to be able to tell our grandchildren about their great-grandparents and what life was like when they were young—what cities and towns were like, and how people traveled before there were passenger planes, and how all females from age twelve had to wear girdles and stockings every day and all men had to wear ties every day and how children used to be able to play in the park and ride bicycles alone without worrying about "dangerous strangers." We can share our family picture albums, which help children to feel part of a much larger clan of truly loving aunts, uncles, and cousins.

We represent the past; we are the family historians. But even more important than that, we now have the greatest gift of all to give when we say, "I understand how you feel" and can really mean it.

❦ 5 ❧

Teenage Grandchildren: A Special Case

THERE COMES A TIME when grandparents, if they don't know any better, suffer a special kind of grief. It is transitory but painful while it lasts.

I can predict the moment with considerable accuracy. It occurs when a grandparent—usually a grandmother—calls and says, "I can't *believe* it! Amanda is rude, nasty, doesn't love me anymore! She was *the most* adorable child, and I was her favorite. The minute she'd see me, she would run into my arms yelling, 'Nana! Nana!' and we always had the most wonderful time together!"

The diagnosis for this relatively sudden change in personality is simple: Amanda is twelve or thirteen years old. We could save ourselves a lot of stress if we would try to remember what we were like as puberty and adolescence arrived. It would also be a good idea to remember what it was like to be a parent when our children reached this crucial time of growing.

According to my own diary, I was hysterical with joy one minute (a boy looked at me kindly) and in the depths of suicidal depression a few minutes later if my parents wanted me to go with them to a family gathering ("They will all treat me like a *child*!").

When my daughter was thirteen I wrote an article for *Parents* magazine titled "The Year I Became a Monster Mother." Wendy's gaze of loathing could make me think I was about to be disintegrated. All we have to do is remember two things: our own past and the power of hormones.

The challenge for grandparents is to try to understand the developmental needs of grandchildren, who may adore us until age ten or eleven and then may not want to have anything to do with us for a couple of years.

Once upon a time we were the perfect grandparents: We were probably more permissive than parents; we were the best storytellers; we had the patience to play Monopoly longer; we were the people who knew games to make children forget their troubles when one of them had the flu. Now, suddenly, this gawky twelve-year-old is embarrassed by kisses and hugs, and given the choice of staying with Grandma and Grandpa when there is a Saturday Little League baseball game, there is no question that the game among peers wins out. It hurts! The special gift grandparents can give their grandchildren is unconditional love, and when the children who have so enjoyed basking in this glow of love for a number of years are suddenly more entranced by other children and larger adventures, we have to recognize that we are expected to make a new adjustment, accept another change in our lives.

I have a friend who is ordinarily a kind, calm, sensible person. After a recent telephone conversation, I wasn't too sure whether she'd had a nervous breakdown; the problem was that she has a thirteen-year-old granddaughter. For almost an hour my friend complained bitterly. "I can't understand it—Dana was such an adorable child, we had such a good time. Now she's rude to me and my friends, doesn't want to spend any time with me— I can't stand her, to tell you the truth. I find myself yelling at her, and she's sullen and acts as if I were her enemy. It's such a disappointment!"

It shouldn't be. Rebellion is a normal transition from childhood to adulthood. It is the way most young people start the necessary battle to move away from the safety and security of parents and family in order to start along the road to independent maturity, adulthood. The safe and more comfortable the relationship to parents (and grandparents!), the harder it is to struggle toward moving away, toward the kind of autonomy that is essential for growing up.

A friend is shocked because her fifteen-year-old granddaughter wants to spend the summer going on a hosteling trip to Europe rather than spending it at Grandma's cottage on a New England lake—something she has loved doing for ten years. Practically every grandparent I talk to goes through the same shock. How could this wonderful, lovable grandchild become angry, unfriendly, even quite nasty and cold? Look at it this way when it happens to you: Your grandchild is still wonderful— and very brave. Nothing could be harder than to give up the comfort and safety of a grandparent's tender and unconditional love. It is just as painful for the young person. It takes courage and fortitude to struggle to grow up. The kids we have to worry about are the ones who remain passive, easygoing, never quite able to begin the tough struggle to get themselves out of that nice, comfortable nest.

When I was about fourteen, my parents and my brother were getting ready one Sunday to visit my father's family in Brooklyn. I said I didn't want to go, I wanted to stay home, I had some work to do. After they left, I became very mournful and guilty.

I wrote in my diary, "I don't know what is the matter with me. I have become a terrible person. I know how my grandparents and aunts and uncles love me, and I hurt my father's feelings. I feel so ashamed and miserable." When I think about it now, I still feel a wave of sadness about something that happened more than fifty years ago! As an adult, I realize my behavior was quite normal; all those relatives loved me too much and viewed me as a child. I was trying to grow up. Once I felt I was an adult, the flood of affection and gratitude returned. I loved visiting my grandparents and so deeply regret that they died before I had a chance to have much time for an adult relationship with them.

Let it happen! Don't fight that temporary loss of closeness. You can remain friendly and caring, but at a distance if that is what your grandchild wants for the time being. You can let the grandchild know you are there if he or she needs you, and you can offer to go to a movie or a play or a basketball game, but this offer needs to be prefaced by, "I know how busy you are these days, but if you feel like it . . ." Don't fight the inevitable! It is foolish to complain. Disapproval only makes matters worse. The worse scenario is saying, "How dare you look at me that way!" or "It's too bad you don't like me anymore." Such comments create an armed camp, which is the last thing you want to happen. I think the best thing a grandparent can do during this period of a grandchild's appearing to break away is to acknowledge it quite directly, openly, so the young person doesn't need to become defensive and guilty. What I expect to say to my granddaughter when she'd rather be dead than seen with me is, "I wish you could have seen your mother when she was your age! She couldn't stand the sight of me for a while! She was just growing up. Now we are best friends. The same thing will happen to you and me." I don't have to tell her that in the back of my mind I am already fantasizing about the travels I had with her mother later and hope to repeat someday with my grandchild!

While I am not a historian, I would be willing to gamble that in all of history there has never been a harder time for growing up. That same diary that I kept from about twelve to sixteen now sounds so naive and innocent. There was never any option in my mind about premarital sex; I had vaguely heard that some musicians used dangerous drugs. I walked safely in New York streets and rode safely on its subways at any time of the day or night. I had never heard the word "mugging," and I'm not even sure I knew what "rape" meant. I was seventeen before I learned about birth control. I can't recall ever hearing anyone speak of abortion and was greatly shocked when my cousin told me her mother—a genteel, Victorian, sweet lady—had had two abortions because it was during the Depression and her husband felt he couldn't possibly support more than the two children they already had. I didn't know anybody who was divorced. I didn't know any adults who were having affairs. I never saw a pornographic magazine, and there was no blatant sexuality in the movies. Looking back, I think I was lucky! It terrifies me when I think of the pseudosophistication of young people today; their cynicism about what we try to teach about values and what they see all around them; and the temptations to experiment with dangerous drugs and inappropriate relationships frighten me half to death.

Even if grandchildren seem to withdraw from us for a while, they need to know how we feel about some of the pressures they are undergoing.

My granddaughter called me one day and said, "Grandma, I need help with peer pressure." Some of her classmates were trying to get her to date boys, some of whom were calling her on the phone. It was wonderful to watch the strength of character she showed in following her own feelings, in recognizing she wasn't ready. A long telephone call with Grandma seemed to fortify her ability to "be herself."

We can have a good opportunity, in the years just before the need to break away for a while, to talk about our values, to listen to what our grandchildren can tell us about the pressures, their fears, their need to be accepted by their peers. We can react with sympathy and show that we are eager to learn from them what life is like in their generation. And the more we really listen respectfully, the more opportunities we will have to try to serve as a bulwark against some of the genuine dangers.

When our grandchildren reach adolescence, we have to accept the fact that there are many things we find hard to understand and there are changes that trouble us greatly, but we have to accept the realities if we want to be helpful and keep in touch. My daughter tells me, "Mom, I know you find this hard to believe, but six guns were found on kids in the junior high school, and there were eight rapes reported in the high school. We can't let the kids go to the beach without adults, or even to the movies. It's just too dangerous." I wonder if you can possibly imagine what town she is describing. The South Bronx? East Los Angeles? No. She lives on Cape Cod, a place where we could not ever have imagined anything but the beauties of nature, serenity, and safety. We need to realize how different the experiences are for young people today.

Of course, younger grandparents may have a much easier time understanding the stresses on their grandchildren. Those in their forties or fifties were surely exposed to a time of tumult and change. The Vietnam War, the Cold War, starvation in other countries, computerization. They were the generation when so many changes began to occur. Older grandparents can use their own teenagers as a point of reference. But what any of us may "know" rationally is often of little consequence. We have a natural inclination to protect our grandchildren from confusion, pain, frustration, and disappointment.

Another thing never mentioned in my diary was concern for the planet! Animals there were in abundance; all water, air, the earth itself were, of course, safe forever. I had never heard of an atomic bomb, of computers that could playfully set in motion terrible destruction. I certainly took trees, birds, and butterflies for granted. I never gave a single thought to overpopulation, I never thought about violence, crime, or fear in my neighborhood.

Surely, terrible things happened while we were growing up—Hitler, the Holocaust, world wars, and the Depression were part of our experience—but I think the big difference from the lives of our grandchildren is that we were hopeful: Things were going to get better. Today's young people are scared, cynical, and bitter about the failure of adults in allowing life to have become so hazardous that we can't even be sure the planet will survive our crimes against it.

The language of teenagers is so different and strange; some of it is amusing, some of it seems to us to be quite disgusting, and much of the time we may be mystified by it. There is a vast difference between taking the attitude "Please never say those words in front of me" and saying, "You have no idea how strange it seems to me to hear you using words that I didn't ever *learn* until I was a grown woman!" We remain close the more that we indicate we want to learn, to share new ways and ideas—but that at the same time we want our grandchildren to know how we feel: that it would be tragic for their future should an unwanted pregnancy occur before marriage. We want them to know that, hopefully along with their parents, we will never reject them and will want to help, but that their becoming more mature involves making choices, sometimes delaying pleasures or avoiding activities that are inherently dangerous or unwise.

Of all the things I never mentioned in my diary, surely the term AIDS is what is most terrifying now for our grandchildren. Again, as partners with their parents, we need to inform, educate, warn very, very seriously, never in anger, always "because we love you so much." Sometimes parents and grandparents may disagree about how much information to give about sexuality during adolescence—I vote for as much as possible and frequently, not merely as information but also as a way of opening up discussions in which all share their feelings and opinions. But if you have misgivings because your adult children seem to give too much or too little attention to this aspect of growing up, it will be necessary to accede to their wishes, although you may try to discuss the issues together, alone. But on the subject of AIDS the dangers are just too staggering and terrifying, and all the adults in the young person's life have absolutely no choice but to provide information, guidance, and a clear message of the possible consequences of careless, irresponsible behavior.

It is hard to avoid taking a grandchild's side against parents as a way of holding on. But there's an important difference between advocacy and mediation. It's a delicate balance, and we need to be aware that we might be able to ease some situations, but only when parents are willing.

Eighteen-year-old Alicia brought home a boyfriend who was twenty-eight, hadn't finished the last year of high school, and was unemployed. Her parents were out of their minds with worry that Alicia might marry Ralph. He was handsome, charming, and definitely eager to have a sexual relationship with Alicia. Grandma invited both of them to visit her over the Christmas holidays in Florida. Grandma did everything possible to be approving and accepting, making Ralph feel comfortable. She never offered a single word of criticism. A few weeks later, Alicia wrote to her:

> Grandma, I'm not seeing Ralph anymore. If you had acted mean or upset, I wouldn't have been able to see him so clearly, but you were so nice to both of us that I began to see he was too

old, too lazy, too immature. I realized I was more mature than he was when you never said a word about his being too old for me.

Sometimes third-party intervention can be very helpful, but only when parents encourage our participation. We have to find the fine line between denial of the facts and terror. The only way we can help our grandchildren fulfill their talents, lead useful and meaningful lives, and set goals for the future is to accept the facts and always try to behave as role models. I think that every grandparent who can ought to be involved in the social issues affecting us all. I buy small pieces of the earth from time to time from an organization called Nature Conservatory. For fifteen dollars you can buy a place where there are several bird nests. I support Greenpeace and other environmental advocacies. I want my granddaughter to know that I contribute to The Fortune Society, an agency that helps ex-convicts change their lives, learn to read and write, have the counseling and the TLC they never had before, so they can become useful citizens. She knows that her grandfather and I both work very hard to help people in trouble, even though we are in our seventies and Grandpa had a heart attack and Grandma had a stroke. We could opt for retirement, but we go on needing to make a difference. We hope this will help to reassure Rhiannon that one never gives up and that each person matters and can make a difference.

Grandparents ought to aim at making teenage grandchildren feel proud of them. For a while we may have to let go, get busy with our own lives, and not pressure grandchildren to spend more time with us. We need to stop reminiscing about how cute they used to be! That doesn't help them move toward greater maturity, at least during these difficult, insecure years of rapid growth. But a most important function during this period ought to be comforting the parents of these children who are having to live through the traumas, the crises of life with adolescents! When I asked one five-year-old what grandparents should do, her mother interrupted and said, "Grandparents should be kind to mothers!" Good advice at any time, but most especially during this difficult time when children move toward becoming adults.

Whatever the age or the upsetting, sometimes frightening behavior, one thing is absolutely essential: Whatever we say to try to explain a different point of view, we must always make it clear we love the grandchild unconditionally. Secondly, we can only be acceptable role models if we try, as they say, "to understand where they are coming from." We need to be good listeners and show we are trying to communicate with them, convincing them that beneath changes in behavior there are still common bonds.

But it's not easy to roll with the punches. Forgotten are the ten thousand games of Candy Land and Gin that we played when they were sick; forgotten are the trips to the zoo and Sea World and Playland. For a few painful years we may be seen as The Enemy because we remind them of when they were young. Today's teenagers live in terror, confusion, and often even despair as they try to leave childhood behind and become adults. It was never easy to live with hormonal earthquakes, let alone a markedly insane world. The best we can do is stand by, always loving and supportive, never relinquishing our values but making it clear we are available for the inevitable crises.

Those once adoring and adorable little children can hurt our feelings. My granddaughter came to visit during Christmas vacation. We took her to see three plays, delivered a cousin to play with her, and took her out for a fancy English tea as well as to an assortment of hamburger places. We didn't get any hugs we didn't ask for, and her parting words to us were, "The seats at *Cats* were awful—I couldn't see a thing." What was the trouble? Is she just a rotten ingrate? No, I don't think so. The trouble was that a period of emotional distance was just beginning. It was up to us to behave as mature adults and refuse to be wounded.

A grandma wrote to me: "I am so deeply hurt. My two grandsons have become rude and inconsiderate. I think I can stand anything but rejection! They would not leave their TV to say good-bye to us or to give me a kiss. It seems to me my daughter does nothing to encourage manners. They used to be so sweet and loving. They did call to apologize later—I'm sure this was probably under duress—but I vowed we would not bother them soon again."

A very poor solution. I'm all for good manners, and I think that when a child of any age hurts our feelings we should speak up and say so. But what I try to remember—and what I recommend for other temporarily rejected grandparents—is that we must expect a certain cooling to occur for a while. The reason is that it is easier to target grandparents for The Great Rebellion, which is healthy and normal as children struggle to leave babyhood behind them. Grandparents may make children feel safe and snuggly when they are very little. Who gives as much time for loving, after all? But sooner or later it begins to occur to healthy kids that this safe cocoon can't last forever; they need to have the courage to resist the temptation to remain safe, and grandparents are safer to forget than parents. We need to respect and admire the urge to grow and change.

But take heart. The time will come when the transition is near enough to completion for the grandchildren to come back to us on a different level, not as cute little babies, but as our almost adult companions. When young people feel more secure, view themselves as having accomplished the task at hand (growing up), we are sometimes surprised to discover that the new relationship may be as much or more fun than the old one.

A grandfather told me, "Sara and I took our eighteen-year-old granddaughter to Europe for her birthday and high school graduation. We had a glorious time. Here was this charming, interesting, intelligent, enthusiastic young woman who was a delight to be with. Rome, Paris, London looked so new and exciting through her eyes. She wrote us a thank-you letter during her first week at college; she said, 'As I start a new and scary life away from home, it is so wonderful to have you as my most special friends. I love you both so much!' We have already forgotten what a brat she used to be!"

6

When Grandchildren Introduce Us to Strangers

Ten or twenty years ago, the letters I received from shocked, outraged grandparents usually had to do with religious inter-marriages: a Jewish grandfather who was sitting shiva (the mourning period) for a granddaughter whom he considered dead because she was marrying a Presbyterian; the grandfather who said, "Never darken our doorstep again!" when a grandson who had been raised in the Catholic religion was going to marry a Buddhist.

Nowadays those causes for suffering sound pretty tame. There are grandchildren who have joined some pretty weird—possibly even dangerous—cults, and if they visit at all they may have shaved their heads and painted their faces blue! Many of us have grandchildren who have had abortions; a grandson introduces us to a pregnant girlfriend he intends to marry although we are convinced she will ruin his life.

And how many of us are truly color-blind and don't think it's time to put one's head in the oven if a grandchild brings home a black boyfriend when we are white, or a white girlfriend when we are black?

It is not easy to overcome prejudices we learned at our parents' knees. As Oscar Hammerstein II wrote in *South Pacific,* "You have to be carefully taught" to hate people who are different.

It may be that the most difficult challenge you have to face as a grandparent is whether you can afford to remain inflexible. That grandfather who went into mourning when his granddaughter married a non-Jew changed his attitude 180 degrees when she presented him with his first grandson! The thought of denying his immortality outweighed the grandfather's attitude.

Sometimes, however, those who are victimized by our attitudes cannot be expected to forgive us. Jean's daughter and son-in-law adopted a Korean war orphan. Jean said, "I'm very sorry. I could never feel comfortable about an Asian grandchild. She's too foreign-looking. Every time I look at her, I can't bear it that they not only needed to adopt a child, but that they didn't show any respect for my feelings." If these young parents don't forget or forgive, that seems reasonable to me.

I believe it is immoral to judge anyone, adult or child, by external appearances. However, it is quite a different matter if grandchildren wish to marry someone who is vicious, or abusive, or psychopathic. Then, along with the parents, we should certainly let our grandchildren know about our fears and concerns, but without anger or condemnation.

Sometimes it's difficult for us to differentiate our prejudices from genuine dangers. One grandmother told me, "It was very hard for me to accept the fact that I was rejecting my new daughter-in-law because she'd once been a go-go dancer." A grandfather admitted, "A son-in-law with long hair and an earring kept me, for a long time, from seeing he was really quite a decent fellow."

Life has changed so rapidly in such a short time. When my parents were young, engagements might well last for several years. Sexual abstinence was the expected behavior, and the young men were supposed to become financially secure before marriage so they could take care of their wives, who would, of course, stay home and raise the children. My parents were the exceptions in those days because my mother was a working woman, but even they were engaged for over a year. By the time most young couples got married, the in-laws on both sides had had a pretty good chance to get to know their child's partner.

Our children usually got married, but many of them are now divorced and may either be remarried or have a "live-in partner." Often they choose to live together without ever being formally married. Something that was once almost unthinkable has become commonplace. Many of us are trying to adjust and accept but don't want to feel required to give up our own point of view, our feelings. It isn't easy, and one of the most difficult problems is that we are usually presented with strangers quite abruptly. It happens with our adult children if they divorce and seek new relationships, and heaven knows we already face or will soon have to face these sudden connections among our grandchildren.

Some situations are so painful—even pathological—that it is hard to imagine a successful solution. Mary is an Irish Catholic whose grandson married a Jew. There is a two-year-old great-grandson now. Mary never spoke to her grandson after his marriage, but now she wants very much to see her great-grandchild. She appears on their doorstep about once a month bearing a large pot of delicious Irish stew. She passes by her granddaughter-in-law, marches into the kitchen, and proceeds to heat the stew; then she serves it to her grandson and his child. "It's as if I am invisible," her granddaughter-in-law says. The couple endure this outrageous behavior because Grandma is a widow and the only living relative of her generation. Her grandson says, "I hate her! I want to throw her out, but then I would be depriving my child of a great-grandmother, when he has no other grandparents."

I am not at all sure this young couple's reasoning is sound. There are some situations that are just too serious. What this great-grandchild may ultimately learn is that Daddy didn't defend Mommy and that she was participating in her own abuse. There are times when finding suitable foster grandparents may be a better answer: the elderly couple down the street, a matching up at a senior citizens center, a friend's grandparents, older people one meets in church.

I don't mean to be unsympathetic about the struggle to change; it's often very painful. In *Fiddler on the Roof*, Tevya, the father of three girls and whose struggle to survive is so strongly based on tradition, expects to choose the husbands. The first daughter chooses the tailor instead of the butcher chosen by Tevya. The second daughter falls in love with a radical on his way to Siberia; Tevya endures—he senses the need for change, the universal hunger for love. When the third daughter chooses a Gentile from the town, Tevya shouts in agony, "If I bend any further, I'll break!" But compassion for suffering is not enough—one has to go on hoping that people can change despite the pain. At the end of the play, even though Tevya can't forgive, he shouts to the villagers his new address in America so loudly that his third daughter will know how to reach the family.

Traditional religious, ethnic, and social values can often be the main factors in dealing with differences. But many more times the difficulty in dealing with a grandchild's choice of a partner represents a hidden agenda, having little or nothing to do with "the stranger."

For example, a grandparent may have unfulfilled dreams of his or her own and has hoped that, finally, a much loved grandchild will live out the fantasy. One's child didn't; the last hope is the grandchild. Or it is possible that a grandparent feels guilty for never measuring up to his or her own parents; this new situation arouses old anxieties, old anger. Some people who have never been able to communicate their feelings to family members unconsciously make "the stranger" a target for the feelings they have never felt able or safe enough to express.

In each situation, it is necessary for all involved to think very carefully before making what may turn out to be permanent—and very uncomfortable—choices.

If we refuse to make any concessions to the new ways, we will probably lose touch with the people we love. Some adaptation seems to me to be the only way I was able to fulfill my most basic value that love must never be sacrificed to discomfort or pride or inflexibility, and that we wanted to stay close to our daughter no matter how different her life might be from our own experience.

Instead of being frightened by the strangers who enter our lives, or having preconceived notions that these strangers are simply too different and can't possibly be suitable companions, we need to look at this situation as an opportunity and a challenge. My husband and I operated on the belief that any young man our daughter brought home from age fourteen on had to have some good qualities or our daughter wouldn't have cared for him. With that attitude—open to the search for goodness—we often got so fond of a particular young man that when he was gone, we missed him more than our daughter did!

How does one do it? A grandchild introduces you to someone he or she may have known for a few weeks, maybe a month, and announces, "This is the person I care for right now." If we are appalled by this relationship, we have several choices. We can make it clear that he is totally unacceptable and *our* parents must be rolling in their graves. We can say we have now been pushed too far—good heavens, this person is even of a different religion or color or social class, or even political party! If this child or grandchild wants to see us, THAT PERSON is not to come along. Or we can say we need a little time and understanding because our background and life experiences were so different, but we are going to make every effort to make this new person part of our lives.

Acting on the latter choice seems to me to be the wisest. It may well be that our grandchild may actually have made a foolish, even dangerous choice. Sending the couple packing means we have no input on how things turn out. By staying very much in touch, without being critical, we make it possible to be present to help this grandchild pick up the pieces later on.

Staying close and welcoming a stranger may, on some occasions, be the only way we can help our loved one begin to see that a particular stranger is seriously neurotic or possibly a psychopath or an opportunist. Even someone in love sooner or later recognizes being exploited and hurt.

One way to go on feeling young is to welcome new adventures, and getting to know strangers can be an adventure as well as a way to maintain a precious relationship.

If we can grow and change, become more flexible, open to differences, we will discover that we are all more alike than we ever could have imagined. All human beings want to be loved, to be allowed to develop self-esteem through being respected and valued by others. All of us thrive on being able to articulate our feelings and beliefs without being afraid of being rejected.

It can be a pleasure to learn about people with different life histories. What better way to broaden our understanding of ourselves and others than to share the broad range of possibilities. This doesn't mean we have to give up who and what we are. We can, of course, celebrate our own holidays, explain our differing religious beliefs, enjoy whatever special advantages we have had in our own lives. Making some accommodations doesn't mean giving up our own identity.

Probably few challenges hit us as hard as facing the fact that a grandchild is a homosexual. A generation ago, few parents were ever told directly that a son or daughter was gay. They surely must have come to suspect; a whole lot of energy was used up in denial, much to the detriment and unhappiness of many homosexuals.

In spite of a slightly more enlightened view in recent years, grandparents are still more than likely to be very upset when the news is out. When we were young, nobody ever said a word about the two schoolteachers who had lived together for thirty years, or about "Uncle Joe," who seemed to want to be a bachelor forever. When we heard anything about homosexuals it was usually that they were depraved or sick or disgusting or promiscuous, or all of these. We, like most of our generation, were ignorant and prejudiced.

Theories about homosexuality were wrong; the observation that homosexuals behaved in antisocial, unacceptable ways was often true, but not for the reasons we were given. Before the closet door began to open, many gay people would have viewed themselves as worthless in some way because this was how they were labeled by society. Feelings of self-hatred lead to self-destructive behavior, whether one is heterosexual or homosexual.

Let me try to persuade you that the world has not come to an end. Homosexuals, who hopefully understand more about themselves and have gained in self-respect, may or may not have full, creative, loving, responsible lives to the same degree as anyone else; what happens will depend in large part on how parents and grandparents react. If you express disgust, anger, or rejection, along with a good part of the rest of society, chances are not too good that this person who wants love and understanding as much as anyone else will become a happy, constructive member of society. If, on the other hand, you learn to accept the fact that homosexuality is not a disease, not even a choice, but is in all likelihood a genetic predisposition, it throws a totally different light on the situation. In every period of human history, homosexuality has existed, and the world has been enriched by the genius of homosexuals in the arts, sciences, government, teaching, philosophy, and all other human endeavors. Gay couples are like everyone else in that some are wonderful human beings and some are not. There are as many stable marriages among gay couples as among heterosexuals. If you can give up the teachings of your childhood and youth, hopefully you will be able to tell your grandchild your love is unconditional.

This is not to suggest that we need feel guilty about being terrified of AIDS, being disappointed about not having grand-children if this is an only child, and feeling strange and uneasy at first. That's normal for our generation.

With more gays coming out of the closet (what a terrible existence it is, trying to hide) and greater sensitivity and understanding by the rest of society, it is now possible for stable, mature, gay couples to adopt children. In fact, some lesbian women are choosing to be artificially inseminated. We need to remember that homosexuals grow up in heterosexual families. The only genuine criteria for having the capacity to be good parents is letting children know they are precious and loved and that their parents will discuss any questions they may have.

One grandmother told me, "My son and his lover are wonderful parents—their two adopted children are the happiest of our grandchildren. Dennis and Tom work harder at doing a good job than our daughter and son-in-law."

After the shock and misgivings and fears, grandparents can then do what they do best by saying, "You are my beloved grandchild and I want to be part of your life for as long as I live."

One letter I cherish was from a grandma who wrote, "I thought I'd have to cut my throat when my grandson brought his partner to meet me. I'm glad I didn't—his friend is a lovely person and takes care of my taxes free of charge!"

When I was young I had a great ethics teacher, Algernon D. Black, a leader of the New York Society for Ethical Culture. He said there were five different levels of possible relationships between people:

> The first level: *Mutual extermination*. "We can't possibly live in the same world—I have to try to destroy you, and you will try to destroy me."

> The second level: *Exploitation*. "I can't stand anything about you, but I can use you, make you my slave, force you to live in service to me."

> The third level: *Toleration*. "Don't bother me and I won't bother you. We will each mind our own business."

> The fourth level: *Mutual appreciation*. "I can accept you for all your talents and enjoy your contributions to the world. I'm glad you are part of my life."

> The fifth level: *Mutual growth*. "I become a better person by helping you fulfill your potential. We both grow to the degree each of us helps the other become all we can be."

I find this philosophy of life essential in all my relationships, and most of all within my family. It is never more important, never more fully tested, than when grandchildren present us with a new person in their lives.

❧ 7 ❧

Grandparents' Rights*

WHEN I CALLED my friend Anne on the phone one morning, we could hardly hear each other for all the laughter and boisterous kidding around that was going on in the background, in her kitchen. "Listen, you ruffians, you keep this up and I'm going to throw that pie right on your heads!" Much laughter, and "Oh, Grandma, you're too old to lift that pie!" I heard, and then more giggling.

I felt like weeping, which may seem a strange response to the joy I was hearing, but I had my reasons. Grandma was seeing her two grandchildren for the first time in five long years of anguish and struggle. When her son had deserted his family and gone to live with a younger woman on a Caribbean island, Anne was as outraged and saddened as her daughter-in-law—to say nothing of being overcome with guilt that in some way she

---

*Research for this chapter was provided by Edith S. Engel.

must have failed her child if he could turn out to be so irresponsible and cruel to his own children. But the rage felt by her daughter-in-law needed some available target, and Grandma was told she would never see her grandchildren. It had taken five years of great patience and courage and enormous legal expense, but Grandma had won. She had endured being vilified by her daughter-in-law, examined by court psychiatrists, patiently moving step by painful step, first being allowed to send birthday cards, then being allowed to talk on the phone Christmas Day, then being allowed to go to a school fair—until finally she was given the right to spend one weekend every two months with her two grandsons, now eight and eleven.

"I knew they needed me," Anne said all along. "They needed to know they were not deserted by me, that I loved them, that their parents' problems were in no way my grandchildren's fault, and that their grandparents loved them and would always want to be part of their lives."

Grandma was right; children need grandparents whether or not there are special problems. And for the first time in history grandparents are turning to the courts, legislators, judges, social workers, mediators, to fight for the right to fill their grandparental roles.

Dr. Arthur Kornhaber, in initiating the Foundation for Grandparenting, expresses the essential feelings of grandparents who are being disenfranchised:

Every time a child is born, a grandparent is born, too. In the natural order of things the generations emerge telescopically, one out of the other. Genetically, every child is the sum of two parents and four grandparents. The child in the womb already possesses instincts, temperament, and emotions that are not his or hers alone. Psychologically, every child develops not only in the world of its parents but within the larger world of its grandparents, of our "father's fathers" and our "mother's mothers."

There is a natural, organic relationship between the generations that is based on biology, verifiable psychologically, and experienced as feelings through emotional attachments.

There are more grandparents alive today than ever before. In the next sixty years, demographers predict, the over-sixty-five population will double. Because of this "graying of America" and the high divorce rate as well as the increasing mobility of families, it might be an era of unprecedented intergenerational strife in an age-segregated society where the aged will no longer command the love, respect, and support of their juniors.

During approximately the past fifteen years, thousands of grandparents have frequently had to fight for the right to be functioning grandparents. These grandparents seek visitation with their grandchildren.

Not too long ago grandparents were traditionally respected, loved, and even emulated. So what happened? Now even if grandparents have no history of abuse, addiction, or obvious malfeasance they are denied visitation as the most punitive form of retaliation by one or both parents. Unfortunately, it has become popular even in families with no apparent alienation for parents to insist on being present during a visit between their child or children and the grandparent or grandparents.

Confused and frustrated grandparents have tried to find some answers to these abnormal restraints. Some explanations offered are:

1. Parents fear grandparents bashing them for their lifestyles, way of raising children, etc.
2. Parents enjoy the opportunity of exercising authority and control over their own parents—a kind of payback. Now the roles are reversed, and the parent is telling the grandparent off.

3. The hidden agendas—childhood grievances, real or imaginary, erupting in adulthood and exercised as denial of an unsupervised visit.

In general the theme is "You did something to me and now I'm sticking it to you."

When adult children and their parents can develop insight into causes and communicate effectively about them, often with the help of a counselor, a reconciliation may take place. Still, a large residue of cases cannot be dealt with except through legal procedures.

Sometimes parents can overreact to single instances of grandparent abuse. One grandmother, speaking in a support group of rejected grandparents, said that her daughter-in-law read a story about a grandfather who had sexually abused his grandchild. Because her father-in-law was somewhat senile, she barred both parents from any contact with the children, although there had never been the slightest indication of wrongdoing.

In another case a grown son recalled being severely spanked as a child. He swore his father would never touch his child and forbade him ever to see his grandson except at large family gatherings once or twice a year under the watchful eye of other adults. This grandfather, who sought the help of a family court, told the judge, "I deeply regret that I ever used corporal punishment on my son. That's the way my father raised me. I thought that was proper discipline. I have since learned that was wrong. I've read a lot and gone to some meetings about raising children. I would *never* hit my grandson." The mediation expert decided, "You may visit your grandson at his home under supervision twice a month!"

In another case an adult daughter became an alcoholic and could not take care of her three children. She asked for a divorce and said she never wanted to see the children again. Her parents agreed she was an unfit mother and prepared to endure the heartbreak of her not wanting to see them anymore either. They assumed their son-in-law would be eager to have their assistance in raising the grandchildren and were shocked when he turned on them and refused to let them see the children. When the grandparents decided to fight the decision through the courts, the reason given for keeping them away from the children was that they were entirely responsible for their daughter's alcoholism, that they had been "terrible parents."

Fortunately, the era for blaming parents for everything seems to be drawing to a close as we have more and more information about the complexity of causes for childhood and adult problems. But this cruel and unrealistic attitude seems to persist in many courts. It is wise to be cautious, but what has happened is that as *legal* experts try to make judgments about *psychological* family problems, their decisions are very often punitive and seldom in the real interests of the children.

Grandparents have sprung out of their rocking chairs to fight back! There are many informal groups as well as formalized action groups fighting for legislation to honor their access to grandchildren. I have in front of me right now some of the publications* now available to advise and support grandparents, and they are excellent resources—not only for attaining information and guidance about how to proceed, but offering support groups through which grandparents can deal with their pain.

One grandmother who has become an expert on these problems wrote:

As a grandchild growing up in the 1920s, the only law with respect to visitation rights with a grandparent was whatever a

*See "Grandparenting Resources" at the back of this book.

family decided. It was assumed that visits to Grandmother's house were mandated routines, as much a part of our Sundays as going to church. It was inconceivable that any other social activity could preempt the commitment.

My mother's generation as grandparents, post-World War II through the sixties, became Mother's or parents' helpers. Now there began obvious differences in childrearing as books like Dr. Spock's and other experts' began to interpret the findings of Sigmund Freud and his followers, which suggested new child-raising practices. The opinions of grandparents were losing ground rapidly. No issues had yet appeared about the rights of the grandparents.

Then, in the sixties, divorces of families with children accelerated to more than 50 percent of the married couples. Territorial disputes between divorcing spouses spilled over to the grandparents. Parents consulting with attorneys learned that grandparents had *no legal rights at all*! What had been taken for granted for generations as the interlocking family now shockingly was without legal and enforceable substantiation.

Parents, according to common law, had unquestionable authority over their children to exclude any one individual family member or all family members they opted to eliminate from contact. Grandparents, contrary to legal tradition, were found guilty of interference in the lives of the nuclear family unless they could prove their "innocence." But there were no laws on the books for grandparents to refer to. Parents had the right to exercise sole authority over their children's lives. Children were in effect the property of their parents much as a car, an animal, or a house. For years individual grandparents felt guilty, ashamed, and alone in this dilemma and felt helpless in personal sorrow and embarrassment. Gradually a few more courageous families wrote to newspapers, called radio and TV stations, learned about each other, and finally consulted with attorneys and their legislators. Very little was known about this aspect of family law. What was known upon research was that there were no laws up to about 1960 giving any rights to the extended family, from the grandparents to the aunts, uncles, cousins, etc. One side of a family, and even in some cases both sides of the family, could be invalidated as far as emotional, psychological, and sociological nurturing was concerned.

It became obvious to the increasing number of alienated extended families that they needed laws passed that would give grandparents (to begin with) the right to petition (sue) for visitation rights in court, ugly and unnatural as it might appear. Emphasis at first was on parents who had divorced. Soon it was apparent that the death of a parent, separation of parents, and even intact families that excluded grandparents had to be included in the legislation for grandparents' and *children's* rights. More and more alienated grandparents joined together, pressing their state legislatures to pass laws protecting the children from deprivation of any and all persons, related or not, who contributed to their mental and physical health.

It has been about thirty years since a number of states passed some kind of law permitting grandparents to petition for visitation rights. In 1981 Congressman Mario Biaggi, as chairman of the Committee on Aging, responded to pleas from grandparents for a congressional hearing on "grandparents/grandchildren—the victims of *divorce*." By this time the thrust of the hearing was for a model resolution that would offer each of the fifty states guidelines of similarity and reciprocity in the event that the parents kidnap the child or children to escape the decision in one state favoring the grandparents to visit. Pursuing the parents from state to state necessitated going to court all over again where the state might have different laws, thus putting the grandparents to expensive trials, financially and physically often out of the question. The resolution was passed unanimously by the House of Representatives, later by the Senate, and then, when put before the National Conference of Commissioners on Uniform State Laws, rejected. It took two years before we learned the reasons, and they are not completely without foundation. The most significant argument was that such matters belonged within each state's jurisdiction, even within the province of the already overburdened, poorly qualified enforcers of family law in particular, because national law could not apply.

There are now all fifty states with a variety of laws enabling grandparents to petition for visitation rights. The American Bar Association called upon attorneys, professors of law, a psychiatrist, and a grandparent activist to contribute to a valuable resource manual that was published in 1989: *Grandparents' Visitation Disputes: A Legal Resource Manual*. Somewhat outdated now, nevertheless it now exists, but it involves a long, expensive legal struggle that exhausts the grandparents financially, emotionally, and physically. By the time there is some sort of settlement the children have also been traumatized, sometimes irretrievably. This is not immediately discernible. After "conditioning" by the parents, the lawyers, or the courts, the kids are often affected as innocent victims of a battle.

It seems that frequently grandfathers and grandmothers differ in the way they fight for visitation or custody. The men are more outraged at what they consider an unwarranted deprivation of what they should be entitled to as "the head of the family." The women, in the beginning, respond more out of feelings of sorrow and bewilderment, but they stay with the effort of reconnection longer and more patiently. Grandmothers, when visitation has been achieved, will make a more determined effort to remediate the harm that has been done to their grandchildren. Increasingly, grandparental efforts in the direction of visitation rights are being recognized by the legislators, with these results:

1. About twenty-five states have no prerequisites for petitioning for visitation rights.
2. About eleven states focus on "the best interests" of the children.
3. In a good number of states, reasons for petition for visitation rights include the death of a parent, divorce, and even when there has been a stepparent adoption, as long as the best interests of the children are maintained.

Further qualifications for grandparents are that they have a stable, wholesome home; that there has been a significant grandparent/grandchild relationship; that visitation does not interfere with the parent/child relationship; if there has been termination of the parental rights of one parent; if denial of visitation has an effect on the child's emotional and physical health; if parents had been unreasonable and denied all contact at the expense of the child or children. But it is still advisable to avoid resorting to legal action wherever possible. Mediation, counseling, and pastoral intervention are preferable, if agreed to, because these alternatives are far less adversarial, less expensive, and less punitive to all.

If and when there is a reconnection between the conflicting parties, the type of visitation varies tremendously with the individual cases. One grandmother won six hours every eight weeks with the two children of her daughter, who had died of cancer when the younger child was an infant.

Two other grandparents were granted two hours in a restaurant every six weeks, with the grandchildren "delivered" by a hostile surrogate. The grandparents took abuse of every kind from the surrogate, and realized he was "doing a job" on the kids before and after each visit so that the two hours were damaging both to the children and the grandparents. Rather than put the kids through this scene, the older couple gave up what the legal system had granted them.

Grandparents Peter and Harriet won the right to have their grandchildren visit them in their home, where Harriet was confined because of illness. The hostile parents delivered the children for the prescribed two hours every three months. The kids arrived and sat silently, refusing conversation, food, juice, etc., until they heard the horn blow for the pickup. The grandparents stuck it out with the help of a support group. Now that the kids are over eighteen, they have apparently distinguished the truth from the distorted tales about their grandparents, and have found to their delight that their grandparents never gave up loving them even when the kids' behavior was offensive and hurtful. If only parents could realize that they are depriving their children of an irreplaceable set of relationships, and in the process often seriously traumatizing the children. Society as a whole is already paying the price for this national epidemic afflicting the family. Just recently, as a result of concerted efforts by grandparent activist groups, there has been a decision in New York State's Court of Appeals that gave the grandparents in an intact family the opportunity to petition for visitation rights. It is not a law on the books but a "case law" (a result of the judges granting permission to petition [not visitation rights per se], but it is precedent-making as it applies to intact families [where both parents live together and obstruct grandparental visitation]). This is a victory for the many grandparents who are excluded because of specious arguments, but it is not the law in New York, and as a precedent for other states may not have any weight.

The successes may be modest, but the data are more and more conclusive that, although the role of grandparents differs in many respects from that of the grandparents of a couple of generations ago, the value of the family as representative of continuity and tradition prevails. Interestingly, even if the parents' generation rejected these values for one reason or another, the grandchildren seem to want to know more about the past life-styles, accomplishments, and mores of their forebears. It's surprising how much they absorb and even how proud they are.

To sum up, it is an unfortunate fact of modern life that the terrible toll of a skyrocketing divorce rate has so often victimized grandparents and their grandchildren. Very rarely there may be some justification for breaking off the relationship, but for the most part the separation is caused by a need to punish some adult, and grandparents often seem to be the easiest targets. Parents need to realize that they are robbing their children of one of the most important and satisfying relationships a child can ever have, and that going through their parents' divorce makes this relationship even more important.

While many states have enacted laws to protect the rights of grandparents in divorce proceedings, grandparents may still have to persist and struggle to remain part of the lives of their grandchildren. "I was scared to death," one grandparent reported, "when that first weekend visit was about to happen. But Stevie and Ken ran into my arms with such genuine joy, it was as if we'd never been apart. Oh, how right I was—how much we needed each other!"

Who shall decide what will be best for the children? I don't think lawyers and judges—or hostile parents—are likely to make the best decisions for the innocent victims of family conflicts: the children. If we are to have new laws about the rights of grandparents when their children divorce, these laws ought to call for the professional intervention of people who are more qualified to figure out how best to meet the needs of the children—skilled mediators, psychologists, social workers, and psychiatrists. That doesn't mean, heaven knows, that every decision will be wise, but there would surely be a better chance. What we need are *child advocates*, concerned only with the welfare of the children.

The most wonderful thing I remember about my grandparents (even the ones who couldn't speak English) is that what I saw in their eyes was a special kind of love no one else could give me. That is *never* to be taken lightly. Except in the most extreme and rare cases of serious pathology, grandparents can be the ties that bind. One would wish that parents, despite their pain, would appreciate this and act accordingly; when they can't, it is time for wiser, calmer experts to mediate.

There are happy endings—sometimes postponed until the children are old enough to separate psychologically from parents and make their own judgments and choices. The best example of this that I know of is when Renee, at eighteen, told her grandmother, "At first I thought you and Grandpa didn't love me anymore. And then I hated you when you made us come to court and all our friends found out and after I got to know you all over again I got very confused because you *did* love me and I loved you. So then I got mad at my father for sending you away. Now I'm just happy. I don't blame anybody. You all did what you thought was right. But now I have a real family, and when you tell me about your lives and the past it helps me figure out who *I* am."

POSTSCRIPT: LEGAL UPDATES, OCTOBER 1992

The U.S. Supreme Court on October 19, 1992, left intact a Kentucky law, similar to laws in other states, that offers visitation rights of grandparents with their grandchildren. The Court did not comment, but refused to review a Kentucky Supreme Court decision claiming the Grandparents Visitation Rights law uncontitutional. The U.S. Supreme Court did not apparently consider that the Kentucky law interfered with parents' rights to raise their children as they wished.

In Connecticut, Supreme Court Judge Charles D. Gill is an organizer for a national task force for an amendment to the U.S. Constitution in protection of children's rights. He maintains that in seventy-nine nations children are protected by their national constitutions. In this country if a child is in the custody of his or her parents, the state has no duty to protect the child legally. The Connecticut organization is:

National Task Force for Children's Constitutional Rights
Litchfield Commons, P.O. Box 1620
Litchfield, CT 06759
Tel.: (203) 567-KIDS (5437)

❦ 8 ❧

Divorce

PROBABLY NOTHING HAS shocked our generation more than the rapidly escalating divorce rate of the past half century. As a child I didn't know about anybody getting a divorce. (I hardly ever heard of anyone *fighting*!) Now we are bystanders as we watch the traumatic events of divorce take over the lives of so many of our children and grandchildren.

How do we handle *our* grief, anger, and shock? How do we deal with the panic we feel that the result of this cataclysm may be the loss of our grandchildren? Perhaps more than in any other circumstance as grandparents, we are challenged to "keep cool." It is an unreasonable and almost impossible task, but a vital one.

I know a couple who went to pieces when their son called and announced he and his wife were separating. There were two grandchildren, five and eight years old. Grandpa shrieked, "No! No! You'll kill us!" over the long-distance line. Grandma rushed to the bathroom, threw up, and said she thought she was having a heart attack (she wasn't). Such dramatic behavior certainly indicates that the grandparents are going to be major problems. But there are other ways in which we can make the situation so much more difficult. Another nonhelpful response is immediately to blame the in-law with such unhelpful responses as, "I *knew* that bum would be nothing but trouble!" or "I told you and told you she was too unstable and neurotic and you shouldn't marry her!"

The first thing we need to think about is that all children love their parents; that they are terrified about what's going to happen to themselves—the most fundamental stability in a child's emotional life is disintegrating. If ever they needed support from grandparents, the time is now.

Often it's not a great surprise; we've been expecting trouble. Just about the worst response we can make is, "I told you so!" What our first response ought to be is, "How can we help?" Sometimes we can't help right away, and we need to respect the wishes of the parents. Their shock, grief, guilt, and disappointment may be too intense for them to share them with us. A friend told me about her terrible frustration when her daughter called with the awful news. There had been no advance warning, no sign that her husband was unhappy. Within a three-week period he had "fallen in love" with a beautiful, much younger coworker. His three-year-old daughter adored him. My friend told her daughter, "Come home, or we will come to you right now." Joanne replied, "No! No! If I see you now I'll start crying and never stop. I have to think about Jill. I'm seeing a therapist. When things settle down we will come to visit. If I see you now, I'll turn into a little girl, and I can't let that happen."

In some cases moving in too quickly may make it impossible for a reconciliation to occur. We can't really avoid taking sides. Because we are so emotionally involved, we may make some serious mistakes. When a precious adult child and grandchildren have been profoundly traumatized it takes enormous courage and maturity to try to be objective.

It is hard to contain one's fury. The departing spouse may fight child support. One departing spouse said, "Your parents can support you."

When a parent suddenly deserts, we are speechless with justified fury. When a departing parent doesn't take responsibility for helping the children understand, his choice is not their fault; when one or both parents fight bitterly and call each other terrible names, we become frustrated and bitter because we are helpless. Rage doesn't help, although I know full well what it is like to try to control it.

But we *can* help as long as we focus our immediate concern on the grandchildren. If we can help them feel that we will never, ever desert them, that we will be there for them throughout the crisis and forever afterward, we will have made a genuine, even a spectacular contribution.

It is normal for us to be profoundly disturbed—there is real pain to deal with. But if we focus on the needs of the grandchildren, at least in the beginning, we can make a difference.

There is more and more evidence, as the children of divorce grow up, that they are almost always left with a residue of emotional disturbance. My suspicions were first aroused when author Jill Krementz was writing a book in which she interviewed children of divorce.* We had each written children's books about the death of a parent, and one day Jill called and said, "Eda, this has come as a great shock, but these children are suffering more than if a parent had died!" We begin to get a glimpse of the havoc of divorce on children when our own grandchildren become the victims.

*How It Feels When Parents Divorce (New York: Alfred A Knopf, 1984).

The January 1989 *New York Times Magazine* featured an important article by Judith Wallerstein, who was working on a long-term project in California; the article suggested very strongly that even after ten or fifteen years the wounds could still be considerable. (See Bibliography, page 197.)

I used to think that my concern about divorce where children were involved was just my being old-fashioned; after all, in all the years of my growing up I couldn't recall a single divorce, and among my married friends, in my age group, a divorce was still most unusual.

I think I was also slow to be too concerned because in the 1940s and 1950s most child experts were saying that, after all, it was better for children to live through a divorce than to live with people who didn't love each other or even hated each other. I think most of us would still agree that divorce is a necessary tool where one of the parents is psychotic, alcoholic, abusive, or plagued by any other truly serious problem. But many of us are now rethinking this point of view. When close to 50 percent of the children in any classroom come from single-parent families, something else has happened. Divorce has become an easy way out—a socially acceptable way to be irresponsible. My guess is that perhaps half of the divorces where children are concerned might have been avoided without trauma to children, if both parents had worked hard to learn to live together, as well as creatively discovering ways to have "separate space" in their lives without divorcing. When I put forth my concern about damage to children of divorce in *Woman's Day* I received more than 300 letters, all agreeing, from divorced parents and from teachers, school principals, and pediatricians.

We have been frightened, unhappy—often terribly angry—when our children and grandchildren have lived through one or more divorces. There is nothing we can do about the fact, but we can help with the consequences. We can intervene by trying to help the grandchildren understand their own feelings. We can communicate honestly, not trying to deny their pain. We can assure them that they will never, ever be alone, that many people love them. We can tell them that their parents love them but may not be able any longer to love each other—and perhaps most important of all, we can tell them they will be strong enough to survive. Talk, read books for children on divorce together, make it clear you are always available to listen to their problems. Often the intervention of grandparents can help to make a child feel safe again.

I think divorce laws should be much tougher. I would make marriage counseling a prerequisite before any divorce could be granted. Custody, visitation, and child support should all be settled with a trained mediator. I have no objection to people without children divorcing easily. But I think we have made too light of the consequences for children.

When there is no other choice than divorce, we can help the children recognize the vulnerability, the emotional problems, of the parent who is leaving. We can explain simply, not belaboring the point, that grown-ups can have "hurt feelings," that each adult brings all his childhood experiences into marriage and parenthood, and that some people are too emotionally crippled to overcome their problems. Love is surely present, and there can be concern and compassion for grown-ups who can't deal with their responsibilities.

When our adult child goes through a terrible divorce and the ex-in-law behaves abominably, it is perfectly normal to have murderous fantasies! One conjures up slow, painful forms of dying, or terrible misfortunes! There is no reason to feel guilty when we are outraged about real injustices. But what we do about these feelings is of vital importance to our grandchildren. We always must remember that no matter how furious we may be, this person is the father or the mother of a grandchild who, no matter what the circumstances, will always love this parent. One grandmother told me, "It's incredible! Jim beat the children, was abusive to our daughter, was a gambler and an alcoholic, hardly ever sends the child support until the court gets after him, and Tracy and Alison love him!" Unless behavior continues to be abusive or dangerous after a divorce, our job is to support our grandchildren's positive feelings for a parent as much as possible. In adulthood these children may have the strength to face a parent's serious inadequacies, but it is too painful in the earlier years. Denial is not always or even often a useful way of dealing with emotional pain, but after a divorce children feel so rejected by the parent who has left them that that's as much as they can handle for some time.

A father told me, "Our daughter and granddaughter came to stay with us for a few weeks after the divorce. They looked so wounded, it nearly broke our hearts. During the visit Jennifer got very sick—I think it turned out to be measles. Our daughter called her ex-husband and asked him to fly down so he could drive them back home. Jennifer needed someone to hold her in the backseat; measles can be mighty serious. That bastard refused to come—he had plans for a holiday. If I didn't hate the idea of going to prison for the rest of my life, I think I could have killed him! I drove my daughter and granddaughter home and took a plane back home. All this happened six years ago. I was sure the rage would be with me forever. I haven't forgiven this behavior at all, but I am no longer obsessed by the memory."

We need to try to let go of those strong emotions that occur in the early stages of the crisis. They interfere with the grandchildren's recovery. We also are likely to discover there were problems in our relationship with our own adult child and our in-law. Long-hidden feelings surface to complicate the situation further.

A grandmother told me, "There were so many shocks when my son and daughter-in-law divorced. I knew that Sherry had never been crazy about me, but I found out she had hated and despised me! I'd been so good to her! She had a splendid job, had a wonderful salary, but our son tried to get custody of our grandson, even though he had lost his job and had been unemployed for several months. Now he not only had to look for work but also would have to hire a caretaker for Billy. He asked Sherry for child support until he could get on his feet, and she said, 'Your parents are rich—they can support you!' We were in our early sixties, worried about retirement and health care, etc., but, of course, we took over."

Having to help to support a divorced child and grandchildren adds to the anger against the ex-husband or wife. It creates so many new problems at a time of life when we expected to have more freedom and to save for old age. Many of us also have aged parents who are dependent on us. To our surprise, due to the rate of divorce and longevity, we have become "the sandwich generation" at a time when we expected to be free of heavy responsibilities for others.

As with so many special stresses of these times, grandparents can find support groups specifically related to divorce. We can't put on a brave front at all times and never complain! The burden is too great. Fortunately, there are so many grandparents caught in the crises of divorce that we can complain to each other and be comforted. The release of hostility, disappointment, and frustration makes it easier to deal with the realities more responsibly. "Well, I got *that* out of my system!" we can say to ourselves, and then get back to the business of being as helpful as we can be.

The only place where we can't explode is with the grandchildren. But sometimes it can become impossible to contain our feelings. A grandmother told me that she and her husband had planned the most perfect Christmas present for their daughter and her three children, who had been through so much pain. It was to be a trip to Paris, where they had many friends, all eager to entertain and house the visitors. Side trips had been planned; there were places the children wanted to go because they had been studying the Middle Ages in school and were dying to visit castles. One child wanted to see cave drawings, because he was studying primitive man. All knew the story *The Hunchback of Notre Dame* and wanted also to visit the Place de la Bastille, having seen movies about the French Revolution. Since their time in Paris would be brief, the plans were made very carefully. The trip would cost much more than the grandparents could afford, but they were so eager to give their daughter and the children a wonderful experience, since they had lived through a year of agony.

Two weeks before the trip, the father of the children remembered there was a statement in the divorce decree that he was to have the children with him Christmas Eve. He threatened to sue for custody if the children went on the trip, denying him his rights. All involved were terribly disappointed, the grandparents outraged and about to lose a great deal of money as well. It was just TOO MUCH! Sometime later, Grandma said, "I can't pretend that I am not angry at your father; we could never be friends. But I guess he loves you so much he can't be away from you at a time that he feels is very important." If Grandma really believed that, she's in line to buy the Brooklyn Bridge! But white lies are unavoidable.

A grandmother wrote to me:

> My daughter and son-in-law are getting a divorce. They have two children, three and seven. My son-in-law just up and decided parenthood and family life were "too much for him" and he deserted his family. Needless to say, my husband and I have only

murderous feelings for him, but my daughter insists that she is working very hard to encourage her ex-husband to continue some relationship with the children because, no matter what, they love him. She forbids us ever to say one word against him. Do you think she is right? Shouldn't children know what has happened? The reason I am so concerned is that the children blame my daughter. She's an easy target. It just about kills me!

I feel very strongly that this daughter is right. My experience has been that young children need a heroic image of parents, and this is doubly true when a parent is absent. All the angry feelings, all the struggles over discipline and rebellion hit on the live-in parent. I think this can be explained simply and quietly without attacking. "Hey, listen, I'm your mother, and my job is to take care of you. It's easier for you to love your dad because you just have fun with him. I understand this, but I'm in charge." This is enough to clear the air.

John and Roberta were married for two years, and by the time they were divorced, Roberta's anger over John's failures as a husband and father of their five-month-old son had reached monumental proportions. Although she had had a warm and comfortable relationship with John's mother at first, by the time the couple separated Roberta's anger had spilled over to anyone with connections with John. She swore she was taking the baby and moving to the opposite side of the country and wanted no contact whatsoever with her ex-mother-in-law.

This was devastating for Marion, John's mother. She understood a good deal of John's problems. It appeared that he was becoming more and more manic-depressive and during his depressions became sullen, hostile, distant. She begged him to get professional help, but he refused. After the birth of his son, it was clear to his mother that he was getting worse; she understood why Roberta wanted a divorce, but was totally shocked by Roberta's turning on her with such rage. Marion told me, "I believe Roberta felt that I had caused John's problems. This was before all the research that made it quite clear there could be a chemical imbalance in the brain with manic-depression and that the proper medication could help. Also, it was not always associated with severe problems in childhood. I was in my fifties when our grandson was born. Having no other children, I knew he would be my only grandchild. Losing him so suddenly left me feeling he had died; I was in mourning."

Marion began to correspond with Roberta. She begged at least for new pictures and news. Roberta began writing back, mostly about being poverty-stricken and needing financial help. Marion said, "I recognized it as blackmail, but I accepted it as my one way of maintaining contact. We paid for Jonathan's day care and summer camp; we sent very generous birthday and Christmas presents—and I was sure to send gifts to Roberta as well.

"When Roberta wrote several years later that she was about to remarry, I wrote how happy I was, offered to pay for the honeymoon, and baby-sit while they were away! By now all the steam had dissipated; I'd picked the right moment *finally* to see my grandchild. That 'baby' is now in college; I have an excellent relationship with Roberta's husband, who was always delighted to know I could help him raise his stepson. You have to be terribly patient to heal some wounds."

I find that many grandparents seldom if ever have to confront the noncustodial parent unless that person is their own adult child. But more and more some level of reconciliation is taking place. One grandmother said, "I can't stand my ex-son-in-law's new wife, but after all, she's my granddaughter's stepmother. I forced myself to meet her."

A grandfather said, "I was sure I'd never speak to my ex-son-in-law again, but after a while you realize there's really no choice. There are school plays and baseball games and graduations—heavens, someday there will probably be a wedding!

I'm not going to miss all that. I will be civilized but keep my distance."

A grandmother told me, "After several bitter years my ex-daughter-in-law remarried. We were invited to the wedding and went for the sake of our grandchildren. Surprise! We found it was obviously a good marriage, and once, long ago, we'd been very close to Gerry's parents. After a few tense minutes we admitted we'd missed each other! Gerry's happy, all's well, we can reestablish connections."

So many relationships can survive with sensitivity and patience as long as nobody tries to rush, push things along too fast. One grandfather told me, "Ten years ago I felt like killing my ex-son-in-law for beating up on my grandkids when he was drunk. This week I saw him across the gym at a high school basketball game. The poison was gone—I even felt a little sorry for the poor bastard, who's still an alcoholic. Time passes, feelings neutralize."

One woman wrote me: "Listen to this. My daughter married a man with three children, who, of course, became our step-grandchildren. We also got to know their other new grandparents, aunts, uncles, etc. Our daughter and this second husband later divorced, but his children and their children stayed with our daughter. The father of all these kids later remarried—well, you get the gist! Figuring it all out—birthdays, Christmas, Thanksgiving dinner—we need a social director!"

Divorce almost always leads to remarriage. Often the grandchildren have a very rough time accepting a stepparent, no matter how worthy that person may be. Loyalty to one's parent outweighs any other consideration about that parent's shortcomings. In fact, the more serious the problems of the noncustodial parent, the more children need to protect and defend the myth of his or her perfection! Often grandparents can be the mediators, the confidantes. We need to encourage the children to be patient, test the waters, understand their resistance—very normal, but not helpful. If the stepparent is making serious mistakes—creating a climate which suggests "You better love me, damn it!" or "I am being so wonderful and understanding, how can you treat me so badly"—a grandparent may be able to suggest more constructive alternatives. And (how awful these days) grandchildren must always know that they can tell us when any truly serious or pathological behavior by a stepparent occurs. We now know that some people marry to have a ready-made family (children) they can abuse. We have to try to strike a fine balance between sympathetic understanding of temporary problems and aggressive responses to genuine pathology.

One of our tasks is to accept our new stepgrandchildren. A parent writes:

> My mother is seventy-six years old. She is having great difficulty accepting the children of her son's second wife. The son has two children from his previous marriage, and his new wife also has two children from an earlier marriage. All four children, a boy and a girl in each case, are close in age.
>
> We ask our mother to treat all the children equally in regard to gifts. She argues it would be too much money. When I suggested she spend half as much on each gift, she wouldn't listen. The truth is that all this is just an excuse for not wanting to deal with stepchildren at all. She resists having anything to do with them. I feel this is wrong—and very sad. Do you agree?

My answer began with "You bet I do!" I understand that many older people have a hard time adjusting to the new realities of family life. There are, of course, all kinds of confused, hurt feelings when marriages end in divorce and new families are created. I understand it may be hard to change, but I believe that this grandmother must be helped to understand that she may lose connections with her own children and grandchildren if she puts herself in the position of being a divisive, rigid, ungiving person. It may be that some family therapy including this grandmother might help, but I know it is often impossible to get an older person to participate in something that seems as strange to her as divorce.

Even more serious is the grandparent who feels unable to accept stepgrandchildren of a different race, religion, or ethnic background. I have no words to describe my dismay. I hope no one reading this book is capable of such inhumane behavior, which represents the most damaging kind of role modeling.

There is one aspect of the increase in divorces that we don't often consider. The truth is that before divorce there was death! Then separation was due to widowhood. Second marriages were commonplace in the early part of this century and all through history. So many women died in childbirth; there were no antibiotics, surgical skills were primitive. Thirty-five or forty was considered a pretty good life expectancy for women a century ago.

In my own family my great-grandfather was widowed with four children. As was common then, my great-grandmother's sister came to this country and married her brother-in-law. They had three more children. My mother's mother died when my mother was four; she and her father went to live with their very extended family. I was never able to figure out which were my uncles or aunts or cousins; frequently they were the same people! When my grandfather remarried I later had to meet all my stepgrandmother's relatives. My grandfather and his second wife had three more children. What was basically different in these earlier scrambles was that people were grieving, not angry. Death was one of the basic realities of life, and you just went on. What I remember best about my childhood is that whatever the complexity of identities, all these people loved each other and loved me. I believe we have to strive for the same flexibility and commitment in relation to divorce.

The death of a parent caused severe emotional trauma in the past. Emotional rehabilitation took a long time, with none of the psychological support systems, the counseling, now available. The job now is to use our new tools to deal with a new kind of anxiety and grieving, with the similar goal that love between people who suffer together and care about each other can be equally healing.

We are having a hard time accepting the fact that now that we live much longer, divorce has become an escape route from unhappy marriages rather than death. If we can become more comfortable with this inevitable reality of life, those who will benefit most will be the children. They are the victims of divorce, not the "perpetrators," and should not be asked to pay the price through the immature behavior of any of the adults who care for them.

It is *required* that we accept what seems to be inevitable, that we support both parents if humanly possible, and that we focus our attention on the grandchildren.

Many grandparents would be only too happy to fulfill these obligations. They were typical grandparents who were afraid of losing touch—and who did. It is unbelievable but entirely true that there are parents who will sacrifice their children on the altar of "getting back" at in-laws, punishing them for whatever they perceive as their crimes, irrespective of the needs of their children. The increasing divorce rate has tended to make grandparents helpless victims of the fallout in hostility, a desire for some kind of retribution. I am not speaking of those grandparents who *should* be barred from contact with grandchildren, even when there is no divorce. There are sick and hurtful grandparents, of course. But that is rarely as monumental a problem as tearing grandchildren away from the unconditional love they crave. Fortunately, this is now a problem being addressed aggressively, with better and better results.

❧ 9 ❧

When Crises and Tragedies Occur

IN A PARENT DISCUSSION group we were talking about both the difficulties and the important satisfactions that grandparents can bring into the lives of their grandchildren. Some mothers spoke of grandparents interfering too much, others were upset when grandparents brought candy and other sweets as gifts. For a few minutes it seemed as if the group was overloaded with complaints until one mother said, "But our children need to know that there are a few people who love them unconditionally no matter how angry they might be at things their grandchildren do." After a moment's pause, she went on:

"When I was fourteen a group of us kids went into the basement of my house when my parents were out and we began to smoke marijuana for the first time. Apparently the mailman smelled the pot and called the police. I was sure my parents would kill me, and when we had to appear in a juvenile court, my grandparents looked as if they would help my parents do the job. But all of a sudden my grandmother gave me hug and said she loved me, and later my grandfather, who was a lawyer, told the judge he was my counsel and shouted out loud, 'I am also this child's grandfather!' I know that no matter what I might do, they would love me, and I think all grandchildren need to have that experience." Often in a major crisis grandparents not only reassure grandchildren but can also give parents some better perspective on the situation.

Another story is quite different. A couple we knew were told that their seven-year-old son had leukemia; the shock was overwhelming and terrifying. Before leaving for a children's hospital specializing in catastrophic diseases, Margaret called her parents, who became instantly hysterical. For the next several months they cried most of the time. Margaret said, "What I desperately needed from them was help. To pick up the other kids at school, tell them but reassure them; feed them, stay with them. What they did was rush to the hospital, cry in front of Robbie, scream at the doctors, 'DO SOMETHING!' I had to ask them for money and baby-sitting, but in the end I got much better help from my next-door neighbors."

We need to support our adult children when they face crises and tragedies; offer the services they need, keep our hysteria for when we are alone. Another couple were faced with the possibility of "infant death syndrome"—the pediatrician considered their one-month-old daughter a possible candidate. The widowed grandfather moved in and slept on the living-room couch, where he could hear the alarm bell, freeing his daughter and son-in-law to get some sleep so they could go on working and caring for their six-year-old. Grandpa came every night, but in the morning he went to work and back to his own apartment until bedtime. When his son-in-law protested that it was too much for him to do, Grandpa said, "I can be a watchdog without being a nuisance."

Heaven knows we worried plenty when our children got sick. My daughter and I were recently reminiscing about the time she got the measles and couldn't stand any light in her room; stark terror. But somehow, because we were in charge and had to do the caretaking, we didn't really have time to get frightened (most of the time). It is quite different with grandchildren. We usually feel helpless; we don't know how to react. We want our children to know how much we care, but the last thing they need is to worry about us.

Sometimes we have to control the impulse to try to help too much; at other times a daughter or a son will seek desperately for our comfort; we may even feel frightened because they appear to become helpless, regressing to the need for childhood security. If we ever battled for power, especially during their adolescence, it may be hard for our children to allow us to take over in any way at all. One daughter screamed at her mother, "Don't start telling us about getting another doctor! I'm in no mood for your advice!"

We have to play it by ear, watch and listen and then respond to whatever message we are being given. A divorced father raising his children pleaded with his in-laws to move in when his son was in a car accident and had to be hospitalized for several months. To the degree they could, they did what he asked, never even explaining to him that they had to hire sitters and housekeepers because one of them had a heart condition and the other was still working.

There is no doubt that there are occasions when you may be very deeply concerned about how the parents of your grandchild are handling a devastating situation. Peter was hurt in a football game at age fifteen; his spine was injured, and he was unable to walk. One day when she was visiting her grandson, Grandma met the physical therapist, who told her that her son and daughter-in-law were interfering with the necessary steps to recovery for her grandson. The parents could not bear to see Peter in such pain, as he was being forced to exercise and move, but this was the only way he could recover. They were protecting him, babying him, encouraging him to refuse to do what was asked of him. Under these circumstances he would remain far more crippled for the rest of his life.

What can grandparents do under such circumstances? First of all, listen; sympathize; state their own feelings once, clearly. After that they have to seek out professional help for the parents, perhaps a doctor who specializes in sports injuries to come to talk to the grandchild and his parents. Far better to have an objective outsider. They might suggest that Peter might be more motivated if they all agreed on giving him something to look forward to—a car at eighteen, a trip, money for college. Ingenuity is important, but one of the things that makes it so hard when a grandchild has a problem is that at a certain point we have to accept the fact that we are NOT in charge. This is true with a child who is chronically ill as well. Chicken soup and games of Monopoly are fine, but major decisions must be made by the parents. When I was a child I had rheumatic fever. Looking back, I feel my grandmother cured me with something I adored, Nesselrode pudding. But it was up to my parents to administer medicine, keep me occupied in bed for almost a year. Grandma was friend, companion, helpful baby-sitter, a comforter with delicacies. My mother and father made arrangements for school at home, gave me jobs I could do in bed. The roles were never confused. (What I'd give for some Nesselrode pudding now!)

There are times when direct interference is necessary: when a child is physically or sexually abused (be sure of the facts!); when a parent is an alcoholic or a drug addict; when a parent has a mental breakdown and has to be hospitalized; if a financial disaster occurs and jobs are lost; when a family faces homelessness. If we have the wherewithal to help, we surely should, and if we can't, we need to explore professional resources for help. Fortunately, there are more and more private and public agencies to help families deal with serious problems, and the best help you can give is to find these resources.

There are many crises where children suffer indirectly. A parent has an affair, there are fights and talk of divorce, maybe even violence. It never helps a child to hear grandparents criticize his parents. Even under truly dangerous, pathological circumstances, children need the love of their parents and still love them. Bad-mouthing the parent who has an affair and divorces, or one who gambles, or behaves in any other improper way deprives the child of a necessary connection. Once in a while it is impossible not to interfere—perhaps even report a parent to the police—but under any circumstances it is important to make clear to the child that we understand his or her loving feelings as well as great sadness and a sense of betrayal, but without ourselves being critical.

One grandmother told me, "My son-in-law had an affair and then announced he wanted a divorce. It was all very sudden, no warning at all. My daughter and her three-year-old son were devastated—it's taken a few years to see any real recovery. I wanted to kill that son of a bitch for hurting them; I hated him with a wild passion. After the divorce he behaved like a bastard, too, but never once did I openly attack him in front of my granddaughter. She needed a father; maybe when she grows up she will see the picture more clearly, but not now."

The death of a grandchild is beyond endurance—but must be endured. Of course, grief and mourning are natural and necessary, but the goal ought to be not to make things any harder for the parents. Marion and Rick had a son who died of a brain tumor at age eleven. Marion was raised as a Methodist; Rick was Jewish, with Orthodox parents. When his parents found out the funeral sermon was to be given by a Gentile friend and that the boy was to be cremated, they became hysterical. The fight that ensued completely obscured the death of the child. Having lost a son and a grandson, the two families also lost each other. No matter how it may interfere with our belief system, our children have every right to seek spiritual comfort in their own way. Rick said, "We had lost a beloved child and were also faced with the hidden agenda of my parents. We had been married by a judge in a civil ceremony, and they had never forgiven us. This seemed to be a new opportunity to let us know how angry they were. I don't know if I'll ever be able to forgive them." Hopefully he will, for the sake of the living grandchildren, but prevention of such episodes depends on grandparents recognizing that they are no longer in charge.

How to handle the torment of a lost grandchild—one's immortality, a cherished person? In the same way I think we need to view all losses—as terribly painful, and allowing ourselves plenty of time to feel our pain and then to celebrate, by meaningful work, the life that has been lost. When all three grandchildren were killed in a car accident because of a drunken driver, all four grandparents dedicated their lives to working for MADD, lecturing, appearing on television, attending trials, working for stricter laws. One grandmother and her daughter are working to try to rehabilitate teenage drunken drivers through paying for counseling so they will no longer be a menace in cars.

Grandparents, who have to deal with grief more often than children and grandchildren, as older relatives and friends die, need to serve as role models. It isn't easy. Family crises, awful tragedies, the breakup of a family shock us and leave us in agony. We have so much hope for the next generation; they are our gift to the future, and they are ours. But courage and acceptance—and then giving added meaning to the lives of the survivors—are ways in which we can be proud to be human. A friend of mine told me, "I have such admiration for my mother. My father died two years ago after a forty-three-year marriage; we have a Down's syndrome baby. My mother has a number of painful ailments; her friends are dying off rapidly. And yet she adores her disabled grandchild, she travels with our older daughter, she tries to help us financially when she can, and she greets each death of someone she loves—relatives, friends—with the determination to fulfill some of their wishes, and work."

We never help when we fall apart. We need to try to see what can be of genuine help, how we can help others to deal with life's vicissitudes with courage and dignity.

❧ 10 ❧

When Grandchildren Visit

THE *SECOND-HAPPIEST* time when grandchildren visit is when they arrive! Most grandparents understand what that means. When any of my friends mention a visit by grandchildren over Thanksgiving, Christmas, or Easter holidays, I know that tea and sympathy and a day or two in bed are going to be required. We all love our grandchildren, and visits are a lot of fun—but they also lead to exhaustion, chronic and severe.

In addition, many of our children are having their children at a later age, meaning we have less energy and tire more easily.

Most grandmothers feel guilty if they get exhausted after playing with, chasing, or trying to control two or three rambunctious children all under age eight. Grandfathers tend to be smarter, less neurotic. "One game of Monopoly," announces one grandfather, "and then I throw them out into the yard!" (On rainy days he commands them to watch television!)

Love and exhaustion seem to go hand in hand, at least when

grandchildren are under age ten. This situation calls for *very careful planning.* A number of cooked meals should be in the freezer. Lunch at a fast-food chain for a few days won't kill them. As soon as possible, take the children to the local library and let each one choose a few books. Buy crayons, paper, a few books of games, and one toy each that encourages dramatic, imaginative play. No finger paints unless it's one grandchild you can stick in a bathtub to paint the tub. (The paints are water-solvent.) No clay indoors—it gets into carpets, to stay forever.

Try to plan several outings: a circus, a puppet show, a movie, a children's play. Consider the possibility of hiring a teenage baby-sitter to do some of the entertaining. Remove all breakable antiques. Before the children arrive, hire someone to do the cleaning up afterward; if we know the chaos isn't going to last, we can be more philosophical and laid-back while it is going on.

Don't overplan. The children don't need to be entertained constantly. There should be quiet times. Plan some physical activities—walking, bicycling, swimming—if at all possible.

It's a good idea, if feasible, to have one child visit at a time. It's a relief to get away from siblings and to have the full attention of adults. On the other hand, children need other children some of the time. After a day spent in our company, our granddaughter said, "It's getting boring!" We agreed and went hunting for other children in the motel where we were staying. An only grandchild might be allowed to bring a best friend along.

If I have made it sound as if visits are less than wonderful, it is because I hope they *will* be wonderful, and this is more likely to happen if we don't overidealize the event. A friend just back from a week of entertaining two lively grandchildren told me, "I adore them. They are wonderful, delightful, bright, entertaining children, but by the third day all I wanted to do was crawl in bed at seven o'clock, read the paper, and go to sleep.

Instead, each night I read to Barbara from her favorite book, all about insects, not a subject that interests me!"

This is a case where love is not enough. Along with the joys of seeing the children is the necessary awareness that they are not perfect little angels. One woman I know lives a life of quiet denial; she is unable to face any imperfections and bears a heavy burden, maintaining myths and pretensions. She "loves every minute of the visits." She never tires of being with the children; they are perfect children. She seems to me to be aging more rapidly than other contemporaries as she works so hard not to see that her grandchildren have the same rough edges, the same excessive demands, the same overexcitability as all the rest of our grandchildren.

Probably the most difficult part of having grandchildren visit for several days or even weeks is the question of discipline. We and the children can enjoy a loosening of the rules; grandparents are supposed to be more indulgent than parents, and special treats ought to be part of the experience. But where health and safety and the rights of others are involved, we can't relax the rules completely. We need to make these basic rules clear from the beginning of a visit. Yes, maybe there will be more cookies than Mom allows, and maybe bedtime will be later, and maybe we can relax standards of cleanliness a little, but nobody is allowed to hurt anyone, and there will be no crossing streets alone, and there will be stomachaches if there are more than two hot dogs at the baseball game, and just as at home, garbage goes in the trash can and not on the living-room floor.

Most of us find the kids enchanting, interesting, fun to be with. The level of enjoyment depends in part on our ability to accept the hazards. We will constantly be told, "My parents never make me wear a hat," or "My mom always lets me have three bags of popcorn at the movies," or "At home I only have to brush my teeth once a week." We can't just be pushovers in order to be popular. Grandparents want to be loved unconditionally, too. It can't be done. Sometimes we have to assert our authority and accept being disliked for the next half hour.

Especially with young children, homesickness is something we need to think about. Unless parents have used this opportunity for a vacation, or unless they live at a great distance, I think we should accept a child's need to go home. The next visit will be much easier when the child knows there is an alternative. If going home is impossible, a telephone call to parents may help, or getting out a map and showing exactly where they are. Or writing to them or making an audiotape, or drawing some pictures for them can usually help. Do I have to say, "Never tell a child he or she is a big baby"? I hope not!

When I was eight or nine I stayed overnight with a friend. In the middle of the night I began to cry and wanted to go home. My friend's mother came in, hugged me, told me she had a special kind of candy that helped with feeling homesick. I sucked on the candy, went to sleep, had a fine time. Years later I realized there was no magic power in the little candy hearts we give children for Valentine's Day; I was more grateful than ever for the tender, loving care that was the real power, not the candy. I have remembered that episode for more than sixty years. Being understood and comforted were what I needed.

Sometimes with older children there can be a real crisis. I remember a time when our daughter was visiting my parents, and my mother lost her temper over something my daughter did. When we came to get her there was a solemn tension in the air. When we got home Wendy said, "It turned out all right—PopPop took me away—we went for a ride." It is important, where possible, for grandparents to share the responsibility, meet the crises, spell each other out.

When I was a child my mother was greatly influenced (along

with other earnest parents at that time) by John B. Watson and Behaviorism. One of his least enlightened theories was that children had to have a bowel movement every day at the same time. I became a victim of my lower colon as an adult, and listened to a different breed of expert—Dr. Spock, of course— who was very relaxed about bodily functions. Wendy went to the bathroom when she was in the mood, and I never kept a record. During a visit to my parents my mother made a big fuss about Wendy going to the bathroom every day and was about to give Wendy some castor oil when we returned just in time. Wendy had been constipated during the whole week. As soon as she was with us, the explosion came.

We need to know the philosophy of our adult children, their childraising theories and practices, so we don't insist on our own, sometimes outworn theories. Most parents today have relaxed standards of speech; they want children to be sensitive to other people's feelings, but they are quite tolerant of slang and some swearing. It is of no use and can hurt a relationship if, too often, our response to something we don't approve of or don't understand is always, "Not in my house can you talk that way!" What might be more appropriate might be to show a little surprise, perhaps, but not to make a big fuss. If the language is really offensive to us, we might say, "I know that younger people don't mind those words, but it makes me uncomfortable, so could you say them in your room or outdoors and not to me?"

Adolescent grandchildren may be curious about other kinds of differences from parental attitudes. What we think about premarital sex; what we think about cheating on unfair tests; how they would feel if we went out with a person of a different race. These are ethical and moral questions, and it may be the better part of wisdom to say, "How do you feel, and what do your parents say?" If we are not judgmental we may have an opportunity to point out how times have changed since we were young—to explain our point of view without indicating that anyone who disagrees with us is wrong. One grandmother told me that her sixteen-year-old granddaughter asked her opinion about birth control for high school students. Rather than taking a stand, Grandma used this as an opportunity to talk about how things change from generation to generation. She talked about the fear of pregnancy, about concern about sex-related diseases. She said there was no penicillin when she was young. She explained different attitudes and social customs. At the end of the conversation her granddaughter said, "We don't worry much about getting pregnant, now that abortions are legal, but now we have to worry about AIDS." Grandma, knowing that she and her son and daughter-in-law had very different attitudes about abortion, just said, "It's a very important subject to discuss with your parents and to think about seriously."

Sometimes when grandchildren visit they feel this is a good time to tell us about intimate family problems we may not know about. If such a personal discussion has to do with child abuse, drugs, alcohol, or frightening economic problems we haven't been aware of, we have to ask the child's permission not to keep a confidence. If it is just a good chance to complain, to vent anger or frustration, we can promise not to tell. We want to be good friends and we can be more permissive than parents. It's fun to have secret confidences with grandchildren—it's a special kind of "palship." My granddaughter knows that when she visits me I am likely to take a very dim view of her school's requirements; that I don't believe in most tests; that I don't think any child has to be good at every subject; that I never passed a math test in my life but depended on the indulgence and pity of my teachers. She also knows her mother would never tolerate such an attitude, that she is very strict about homework and grades, probably because we were too permissive when she was young. Rhiannon knows that I'm allowed to comfort her but that I respect her mother for being more realistic and firm than I was. Having differences is to be expected and can do no harm as long as parents and grandparents understand the difference in their roles and respect each other's feelings.

Nothing helps more to cement a more tender relationship between grandchildren and grandparents than visiting without parents. We marvel at the wisdom of the things the children say; we are touched by their concern for a pet, for disabled children; we are fascinated by their insights about politics. What fun it is to see this much-loved child emerging as a person. Laughing together, crying at a movie, eating a disgracefully luscious ice cream sundae, finding out you all love the Tolkien stories, sharing a child's special dreams; such visits bring enrichment and joy, despite fatigue afterward. The only real potential problem is glorifying visits to such a degree that nothing can live up to our expectations. Not for the children, either. Sometimes at the end of a visit it can be a good idea to acknowledge cheerfully, "Well, I love you so much and am sorry there were some disappointments. Maybe next time it won't rain so much and we won't get so annoyed and you will probably win our next chess game." Not feeling a need to deny reality and always being able to celebrate future possibilities is the name of the game.

~ 11 ~

When Grandparents Are Raising Their Grandchildren*

I CONFESS THAT I had never given much thought to grandparents raising grandchildren until the Gulf War, when suddenly grandparents were catapulted into this role by the insanity of the military and the government, which brought members of the Army Reserves into active duty without regard to what this might do to young children, either with both parents called up or at least young mothers. It had never occurred to me that there were no "mitigating circumstances" that would protect young children from being sacrificed to the military now that women were playing as active a role as men.† The scenes on television of little children crying, hanging on to their parents, and being torn away, alerted me to a problem that upset me greatly.

*Research for this chapter was provided by Edith S. Engel.
†During the Second World War, fathers of young children were deferred even if their wives were full-time mothers.

The trauma for the children was very clear. I am sure many of them wondered what they had done to make their parents leave them; that's how little kids think. There was little or no advance preparation—the shock of separation must have been so devastating that I am sure some of those children haven't yet fully recovered, several years later.

My second concern was for the grandparents, who suddenly found themselves fully responsible for the care of young children—all over again.

Grandparents suffer in many ways. Goals and dreams for travel or moving are forgotten. With no energy left over after caring for the children, social life and recreation come to a standstill. Friends disappear when there is no time for doing things together.

One grandfather said, "We've given up all our dreams of an easier, quieter time of life. Now I'd settle for a lunch date with my wife."

Interviewed on television a few weeks after the fact, many grandparents looked exhausted, haggard; most were putting on a brave face, although they not only had to deal with their own stress but also with seriously disturbed children.

Since that time I have become better educated; now I know this relationship is far from uncommon, that at least three million grandparents are raising their grandchildren. There are certainly many more cases that haven't come to light. In some subcultures this role is considered quite normal and occurs frequently. Many times it may be the result of teenage pregnancies where the child-mother can't deal with childraising. It occurs most frequently when the child's parents are alcoholics, drug users, or are abusing the children. One million are children of divorced parents. Many cases occur where there was no marriage and the husband is not in the picture.

One inevitable problem is that roles become confused. Are

these "parents" who must discipline and take full responsibility for the care of the children, or are they grandparents who are so often more indulgent and permissive? It is hard enough to raise children when we are young; the task for grandparents is a lot harder. Fatigue can be a major source of frustration, and often these grandparents have to deal with children who feel rejected and abused and are very hard to handle; they may be very angry and rebellious. No longer (or never) feeling loved by parents, they tend to "act out," testing their grandparents to see if *they* love them enough to put up with difficult behavior.

In addition to the emotional hurdles and the physical stress, the legal system and governmental agencies seem bent on making the situation as difficult as possible. There are thousands of grandparents who want to raise their grandchildren when the parents cannot take the responsibility but who lose out to child welfare agencies and courts that decide the children should be in foster homes. The foster care bureaucracy in this country has become monolithic due to the number of children without adequate parental care, and a child's genuine needs often become lost in the confusion.

In some cases grandparents may end up with more responsibility than they can handle, and at the other extreme they may be shoved aside unceremoniously. Certainly the special relationship grandparents can have with grandchildren in a stable family is diminished as they take on the role of parents.

There are surely grandparents who raise grandchildren with joyful acceptance. In most cases these would be younger grandparents and those who are accustomed to this role within their own social-cultural environment. Frequently the parents ask the grandparents to take over; often a single parent may live in the grandparents' household, but he or she is working full-time or may be unable to carry the parenting responsibility. Because of crime, overcrowded schools, and housing problems in American cities, several women I know have sent their children to live with grandparents on the tropical island from which they originally came. It is easier to be a custodial grandparent where there may still be extended families to share the work of raising young children.

The most serious problems occur when families have to deal with the courts and social agencies. State and federal laws vary greatly and are inconsistent, often being at the mercy of individual courts, judges, and social workers. Many grandparents who would like custody are rejected in favor of foster placement, even adoption, of their grandchildren.

What often occurs is that even in the face of clear evidence of maltreatment of children, the courts, in justified concern for parental rights, will bend over backward and leave abused and rejected children in parental custody. Sometimes custody will be denied grandparents because one parent will, to hurt the second parent, say the grandparents are "no good."

Maria has two children, is divorced, and is living with a younger man who "can't stand it when the baby cries." The children's grandmother is terrified that he will hurt—maybe even kill—the baby when he is in a rage. She reported him to the police. He retaliated by saying the grandparent was a liar and a drunk. As a result, she was unable to get legal custody and eventually, as the home situation deteriorated, the children were placed in separate foster homes and were made available for adoption.

It is a herculean task for grandparents to prove that "the best interests of the children" would be best satisfied by legal grandparental custody. Where young children are concerned the judicial system is antiquated and overwhelmed by numbers; often untrained personnel are trying to deal with the most complex family problems.

Criteria range from "any person who has in reality provided

a stable and wholesome home for the child or children" and is a "fit and proper person, true and sufficient" shall be awarded custody. At the other end of the spectrum are states that allow third-party custody only in the event of a parent's death, other conditions to the contrary notwithstanding.

Changes in the character of "the American family" have gradually led, with the increase in grandparental activism, to the need for laws recognizing the rights of grandparents to petition for custody. As family law becomes more appreciated nationally, state lines and boundaries of residence in different states make it even more necessary for congressional support—laws which will define the possibilities very clearly. As grandparent support groups become more vocal the momentum accelerates, and hopefully it commands the attention of the legislators.

The success of grandparental custody depends in good part on the age, health, and financial resources of the grandparents to deal with unanticipated demands on them. There are grandparents in their forties, in good health, sometimes both still working, who are eager and "able to do it again" and "do it better this time." When the grandparents are fifty-five or over (seniors), sometimes in poor health, with modest nest eggs for retirement carefully acquired after they've seemingly launched their children, it isn't easy to shift gears and go in another direction in life. Often, too, there is minimal if any support— financial, counseling, or otherwise—available to custodial grandparents, either through the individual state or the national government. How many of that older generation who live on Social Security, perhaps at the poverty level, can pay the additional medical expenses and food and clothing expenses and have the physical room to accommodate several additional residents? Some lawmakers have recommended legislation sponsoring tangible support for family preservation for these unanticipated demands on grandparents with new and critical problems. Resources where grandparents can get help must be developed where grandparents can turn for aid in meeting these changing roles. A rescue operation is needed for those children here and now. The alternatives are formidable.

Among other problems is that unless there is legal custody, a parent can validly try to get a child back at any time. Judges and courts are completely unpredictable. In situations in which children are tossed back and forth as the struggle persists, even for years, they don't know where they belong and may constantly have to change schools and neighborhoods, adding to their inner emotional turmoil.

Sometimes when grandparents are asked to raise a grandchild there are unexpected complications. One grandmother wrote:

> Our eighteen-year-old granddaughter asked if she could come and live with us, since she wasn't getting along with her mother. We have always had a warm and loving relationship and we were very pleased at the thought of having her company, but very quickly we could see why our daughter couldn't handle her. She has a job and she does get herself to work. But she spends every cent she earns on fancy clothes, goes out until all hours of the morning, never offers to help with any household chores. She drinks too much and smokes, and has one boyfriend after the other. We are at our wits' end about how to discipline her.

Another kind of predicament occurred when grandparents in their midsixties found themselves called on to raise their one-year-old grandson. Their daughter had become addicted to cocaine, their son-in-law deserted while she was pregnant, and it was clear that their daughter was unable to provide proper care for her child. They tried to persuade their daughter to go to a rehabilitation program, but she refused. The baby was born addicted, which created additional problems. Their daughter was constantly threatening to take the child away from them if they didn't give her money for drugs. Having already raised three children and both having worked very hard, these grandparents had been looking forward to retirement, to be able to pursue interests they had never had time for before.

On the other hand, some custody struggles work out to the satisfaction of both grandparent and grandchild. A very remarkable widowed black grandmother who is a diabetic amputee persisted in trying to obtain custody of her ten-year-old grandchild, whose parents were addicted and abusive. Grandma and granddaughter Delphine spent many wonderful hours together when allowed. The courts at first refused the grandmother custody because she was incapacitated, although she held a responsible job with a modest income. A foster home was recommended. Delphine adored her grandmother and proved demonstrably that she could be helpful with chores her grandmother found difficult. Perhaps because for years the black population has accepted the role of parent and grandparent interchangeably without legal fussing, and been successful at it, temporary custody was granted. Delphine's devotion to her grandmother was a factor in the decision of making temporary custody into permanent custody. Today Charlotte, sitting in her wheelchair, enjoys Delphine, who is fulfilling her dream as a professional ballerina. Grandma Charlotte exchanged her sewing abilities on the school's ballet costumes for ballet lessons that Delphine had longed for ever since she was a toddler walking on her tiptoes.

As with any family constellation, there are wonderful outcomes of custody as well as serious problems: One set of grandparents pursued their deceased daughter's children for years from state to state when their father fled with them every time the courts awarded them to the grandparents—hardworking, highly intelligent, middle-class citizens who went into debt as the years passed. As a consequence of the grandchildren being moved from location to location and from school to school during their earlier years, the grandparents found themselves being blamed for all the grandchildren's problems. Custody was never concluded; the father and the grandparents were in and out of the courts. The grandparents tried to offer the children the stability, nurturing, and continuity the children were obviously not experiencing when they were with their father. When the grandson was old enough to seek out his grandparents on his own and asked to live with them, he was like "a hungry homing pigeon coming to a warm resting place." His motivation to achieve caused improvement academically, and his behavior changed from resentful to outspokenly appreciative. He also learned more about how and under what circumstances his mother had died, distinguishing truth from his father's distortions.

Sometimes waiting, being patient, indicating clearly one's genuine love and concern can make a far greater impression than we think. It is never too late to help when this becomes a possibility.

Sometimes grandparents can be so eager to hold a family together that they opt for custody under very unrealistic circumstances. A grandmother fought like a tigress for her abused grandchildren. Her husband did not discourage her; she wrote the letters, sought help from the courts, her legislators, and any individual or organization that would listen to her until *she* won custody. The kids had been severely abused, both physically and emotionally. The grandparents changed their entire way of life when they were awarded custody—they bought a house, using their savings to provide a nurturing home for the children with every measure of devotion and sacrifice they could. It was too late for the now rebellious, resentful, manipulative grandchildren, who used every trick in the book to thwart the authority of the desperate grandparents. They defiantly ignored

any discipline—they took drugs, dropped out of school inter-
mittently, refused to help in the house (do anything about their
rooms, laundry, cut the grass, shovel the snow, etc.), and gen-
erally were unwilling to accommodate to the new ways of living
with stable family values. Both grandparents suffered serious
illnesses, financial hardship, and heartbreak. Now over eighteen,
the grandchildren have resumed a relationship with their abusive father, who has remarried (their mother died of cancer).
Can anyone advise grandparents not to undertake such an impossible job?

A separated mother with two children, ages two and five, was
dying of terminal cancer. Her husband had been having an affair
for a year and was battling against child support. Forced to take
care of the children while his wife was in the hospital for chemo-
therapy treatment, he shouted at her, "You're a shitty wife and
mother!" She was desperate to make plans for the children after
her death. A sister had four children of her own and said she
could not handle two more. Her parents, who lived in a retirement community in Florida, were her only resource. She asked
to see the hospital social worker, who contacted child services
in the city where the grandparents lived, and a plan was worked
out whereby the child support would be given to the grandparents, a housekeeper would be supplied by a local agency,
and a day care center would take the children for six hours a
day. The mother said, "Now I can die in peace, knowing the
children will be with my parents, and the burden won't kill
them!"

The problem is that there are few situations in which such a
careful plan can be worked out ahead of time. And the death
of a parent changes the picture for both the children and the
grandparent; there is less conflict about choice—we tend to do
what we have to do.

Another situation occurred when the emergency was urgent.

The grandparents in this case were called by a child protection agency. Neighbors had complained—their alcoholic daughter was abusing her two young sons. If the grandparents would not take the children, they would be placed in a foster home, and possibly not together. It is hard to think about long-term consequences in such cases.

A grandmother battled her drug-addicted and incompetent alcoholic son-in-law for custody of her grandson. By the time he was ten he had seen his mother overdosed, pass out drunk, crack up her car, and shack up with a variety of lovers of questionable character. The grandparents are pillars of the community, college-educated and religious. Now, ten years later, both grandparents are ill and are still trying desperately to be there for their grandson, who has learning problems and probably suffers from fetal alcohol syndrome. Their strength and resiliency are constantly being tested because they see the potential in this often creative boy, who needs extraordinary patience and love. These aging, physically diminished grandparents have difficulty fulfilling the needs of this grandchild. Grandparents and grandson are in jeopardy.

There surely are occasions when grandparents have to refuse custody, painful as that may be. Both emotional and physical disabilities have to be considered. Raising children in an environment where grandparents are unable to deal with inevitable problems is no help to the children. Living on little more than Social Security makes custody impossible. One alternative may be to ask another adult child to take the children and then help as much as they can with visits, baby-sitting, and some financial help. Another possibility is to ask the court to declare them "foster parents" so they can have both guidance and financial help, as is available to other foster parents. Applying for welfare assistance through aid to dependent children may be possible. With counseling on such issues as discipline and extra money for necessities, some grandparents may be able to manage.

Whatever the solution, grandparents who can't help are likely to feel guilty and sad. All one can do is deal with the realities, help in ways other than custody, and most important, keep in touch with the children and assure them that they are loved and are in no way responsible for their distress.

For grandparents who assume custody, feelings of ambivalence are normal! No matter how much they love their grandchildren, these grandparents have a tough, exhausting, sometimes discouraging job. Counseling is an important avenue for help. Perhaps family therapy will help. The idea is to discover as many outside resources as one can to support a difficult task.

It seems clear to me that grandparents need far more help than they are now receiving. Henry L. Barton, a school principal, wrote in *New Horizons,** "There should be the same cooperation between the school and the grandparent as there is between the school and the parent."

I would go further than that: Schools ought to provide *more* help to grandparents for whom the financial, physical, and emotional burdens come at what in some ways is an inappropriate time of life.

When the burdens of custody become overwhelming, grandparents need to seek as much help as they can get. There are workshops and support groups in most communities; there are private and public family counseling agencies. There are books to read, lectures to attend. For example, *New Horizons* is a publication of an organization called Grandparents Reaching Out. One of the good things that has happened in recent years is the way in which people with similar problems and challenges have reached out to each other; this publication can be helpful

*Vol. I, No. 1 (April 1992).

to grandparents raising grandchildren. For more information, the address is:

141 Glensummer Road
Holbrook, N.Y. 11741

Other resources and the Bibliography are given at the back of this book.

The most important ingredients for making grandparental custody work are:

1. Clarifying and insisting that custody is legal and permanent if any other solution is considered dangerous.
2. Remaining flexible if a parent or parents become able to care for their children.
3. Never lying; helping the children understand what has happened to their parents and that *in no way* are the children *ever* responsible for the failings of the adults.
4. Grandparents do not have to pretend life is perfect! Ambivalent feelings (of both grandchildren and grandparents) can be endured as long as people can express their feelings. One six-year-old said, "Sometimes we love each other and sometimes we hate each other. Grandma says that's normal." It is!

❧ 12 ❧

Three Generations
Living Together

AT ONE TIME—certainly until the beginning of the twentieth century—it would never have been considered unusual to have children, their parents, and the grandparents living under one roof. Often these households would also include aunts, uncles, cousins, and great-grandparents. One of the most significant sociological changes has been the movement away from family farms, rural life, and farmhouses that could accommodate everyone—in fact, that made good use of everyone's energies and talents.

Even in cities most of us can recall stories of our parents and grandparents living in extended households. My father, a little immigrant boy, slept in a bed with several brothers, an uncle, and a boarder from time to time, in a tenement along with parents, brothers, and sisters. My mother grew up in a brownstone—three floors and a basement—with her father, her grandparents, aunts, cousins, and a "maiden aunt" who took care of the children and did all the family sewing. Some of my most profound memories are about the two or three years when I lived in a brownstone with grandparents, aunts, and uncles.

Nowadays these extended households are less common. It started with people living in small apartments and better economic conditions for the earlier generations of immigrants. With recent new waves of immigration and dramatically increasing poverty and unemployment, it is probable that more and more families are doubling up once again.

The range of circumstances is as great as there are people with different expectations, personalities, needs, and resources. When I worked closely at one time with The Fortune Society, an agency for helping former convicts have an opportunity for rehabilitation, I interviewed many of the people trying to turn their lives around. When I asked if there had been any source of comfort and security in otherwise frightening, turbulent, painful experiences—often no fathers present, mothers working, neighborhoods of prostitutes, pimps, drug addicts, and drug sellers—I got quite accustomed to one frequent answer: "I guess my grandmother—she lived with us."

For some grandchildren, live-in grandparents can be sources of special caring and attention. For other children, having to share a room with a grandparent; having too many people with too many different rules; having to behave differently with a grandparent than with parents; being uncomfortable about bringing friends home; becoming preoccupied with old age, perhaps with illness; and perhaps most of all, being caught in the crossfire of "too many cooks!" can be extremely difficult. Or, if parents are both working long hours, a grandparent may be the only one available for reading stories and playing games.

There are no easy answers; each situation is different. But one thing seems quite evident: If three generations are to live together, it is likely to work out more successfully if it is thought out in advance as much as possible. The advantages and disadvantages need to be carefully weighed. Is a widow who feels lonely and bereft better off living with her children and grandchild, or will the sacrifice of privacy and independence be too great? Is the comfort of having a well-known and well-loved baby-sitter for working parents a good idea if Grandma or Grandpa or occasionally both grandparents have very strong opinions about childraising that, helpful or not, are opposite to those of the parents?

Here are some sample letters I received while writing a column for *Parents* magazine:

> My mother-in-law is moving in with us; we are a young couple in our thirties and have a three-month-old child. My mother-in-law will care for the baby forty hours a week. She is old-fashioned and readily offers unsolicited advice. She has worked as a nanny. Of course, my husband and I will lose much of our privacy, but mostly I am afraid I will lose my son, since he will be under her care so much of the time. She is very energetic and I am afraid will take over my home. I feel very insecure and threatened. I want to overcome these feelings and appreciate the benefits of our living arrangement. How can I confront her with my misgivings without hurting her feelings? My husband is not sympathetic to my concern.

The immediate issue is not to "confront" her but rather to *talk* to her! It is important to set some guidelines at the very beginning of a new living arrangement. Grandma needs to be told what a break this is for the parents, and they know their son will get loving care while they go to work. The parents have to try for real honesty, explaining that they feel young and unsure of themselves but that they want so much to have a very close relationship to their child. Asking advice from Grandma about how they can work together in the most comfortable way will help her to feel more cooperative.

It is helpful to make some definite plans, such as the fact that Mother wants to be in charge when she comes home from work until the child goes to sleep. And that on weekends the parents want to spend time alone with their child. Perhaps the parents can take the baby with them on weekend trips. These are times when Grandma can rest, visit her friends, do things she enjoys. Grandma needs permission to be frank and tell the parents what she thinks. They will need to work out a schedule of other responsibilities, trying to decide which chores each person prefers. The more one shares honest feelings, the more aware each person will be about what is appropriate behavior.

And on the opposite side:

> I am a fifty-five-year-old widow. My daughter is thirty and has just taken a full-time job. She wants me to move in with her and take care of her children (who are four and six) when they're not at school. I love my grandchildren—and the arrangement would certainly be easier on us both financially. But I'm a little reluctant to give up my own apartment and my independence. What do you think?

It is wise not to do anything drastic! This grandma should not give up her apartment until she tries out the arrangement for several months, at least. In making plans for living together it is a good idea to make flexible arrangements, open to change if necessary. Fifty-five may seem around the bend to one's daughter, but it isn't. Grandma needs to think long and hard about the things she still likes to do with her own life—and there is plenty of living ahead of her.

For some women taking care of young children can be refreshing and satisfying—returning, perhaps, to a role they loved best in the world and have missed. For others, there may be a sense of relief that childraising days are past, and much as they may love their grandchildren, they have no desire to live with them. Some adult children and their parents are able to live together and accommodate themselves to each other's needs; in other cases, trying to live under the same roof may destroy what might otherwise be an excellent relationship. Some people feel happiest living in a three-generation household; others need a kind of independence and privacy that just isn't possible in such circumstances. These are the issues one needs to explore during a period of experimentation and introspection.

Sometimes, of course, there doesn't seem to be any choice. Grandma dies, Grandpa has never lived alone, has no idea how to take care of himself, must sell his home because he has no money saved for imminent retirement. However plans may change later, right now he is in a deep depression. His daughter feels she must bring him into her home. The only place for him to sleep is in the room with his nine-year-old granddaughter. She feels invaded, embarrassed; he snores, gets up several times a night to go to the bathroom, complains the room is a mess— he has no place for his own clothes and other possessions.

It appears as if there are no choices, but there are many; wouldn't it be better to give up a TV room or the dining room or an open porch that can be closed, and make some other room his bedroom?

If Grandpa is seriously depressed for several months, his daughter has the choice to insist that he see a doctor for medication, and join a widowers' support group or receive some grief counseling. The family has the choice of finding ways to help this man do things that will help them and make him feel needed and useful. A friend told me she was terrified of her father moving in, but after several sessions with a counselor he began doing something he'd always loved but had never had time for before: woodwork and carpentry. He rebuilt a broken-down deck, made some needed shelves, and built a picnic table, and while his grandson raked the leaves, he held the garbage bag! What happens when someone is encouraged to take another crack at living and knows his life can be helpful to others is that grief recedes. We always have some choices, even in a difficult situation. What to do about the snoring, if there is really no other place for Grandpa to sleep, might be to separate the room by high shelves or a sliding door and give the grandchild some earplugs. She needs to feel that her privacy is important. Maybe Grandpa's belongings can be in a closet in another room.

In general, anticipating problems is better than being surprised. And preparing should always include the clear understanding that nothing will go perfectly smoothly! There is nothing wrong with having some arguments, some differences, some inconveniences, some hurt feelings and frustration—after all, these are part of life. Whether one can survive depends on whether everybody tries to deny such feelings or accepts them from the outset, saying such things as "Listen, the truth is we're both bossy and opinionated. Let's say the kitchen is yours on weekdays when you're home with the kids and we come home too tired to cook. On weekends, the kitchen is mine!" Or, "Listen, Dad, you know how I feel about my tools; it will drive me crazy if you fool around with my worktable in the garage. Hell, you taught me all that stuff, and *I* do the fixing." Maybe Grandpa could be encouraged to offer his services to a neighborhood school, teaching kids about shop, all the "stuff" he once taught his son. Or maybe the local adult school would be happy to have him teaching adults how to fix things in their homes. When negative feelings are aired in a civilized and caring way, it is much easier to live with ambivalent feelings.

One of the major problems in joining forces depends on whether there is "old business" lurking beneath the surface that needs to be dealt with before the living together takes place. Mother still harbors some discomfort because her son-in-law is of a different religion than her daughter; maybe their civil wedding ceremony made her very unhappy. Maybe a daughter re-members all too clearly some very serious conflicts with her now widowed father when she was a teenager. Maybe a moving-in parent is extremely thrifty and feels her son and daughter-in-law spend money too freely. Maybe a son feels his father favored his two older brothers when they were children. All need to think seriously about some hidden agenda that is lying dormant but that may surface under new circumstances.

It is important also to think about things that may change as time goes by. In one case, Grandma was healthy and vigorous when she came to live with her daughter, son-in-law, and two grandsons. Her daughter had an exciting, glamorous job that involved very long workdays and some evenings as well. It looked like a perfect setup to have Grandma take care of the children and do the cooking. But then she had a heart attack and needed care herself; when she died, her daughter found a note from her mother: "You have been more than a mother to me." Her daughter told me, "She died before she realized I was almost at the end of my rope!" What had seemed at first to relieve her burdens had become a heavier burden than ever before. It is wise to anticipate such things as illnesses, general problems of aging, the difference when children become teen-agers and don't want the care that was once wonderful but has now become smothering. The only thing we can anticipate with certainty is that life circumstances change!

Differences in personality are very important also. Two rel-atively cheerful, calm women can learn to share household activities. An introvert and an extrovert may have a hard time communicating successfully. A person who is comfortable with playing a dependent role will find it easier to live with a "take-over mother-in-law."

Probably the best idea when contemplating a three-genera-tion household is for all members of the family to spend a little time seeing a family counselor who can help to assess the likelihood of whether this arrangement will succeed. But even with expert advice there may be unexpected problems. Many years ago, one grandmother told me, "I thought I would love living in a beautiful suburb in a big house, with trees and flowers and quiet. But all my life I lived in a crowded neighborhood in an old apartment building in Brooklyn. The butcher was my friend, the new people who moved in, mostly from Puerto Rico, had many children, and I became their Jewish grandma! Everybody was my friend, neighbors talked to each other every day. In the fancy suburb nobody talks to anyone. There were no buses to go places; I felt like a prisoner. My son had a fit when I said I wanted to move back to Brooklyn; he said the neighborhood wasn't safe, I might have to walk up steps, people were killing each other in the streets. I never had any trouble. Old and new neighbors loved me. I never played bridge in my life and I never wanted to! The woman who cut my hair, I knew her since she was a child, she charged me ten dollars. In the suburb my daughter-in-law had to drive me to this fancy "hair salon"—I couldn't believe it—forty dollars for a haircut!! I only wish I had held on to my apartment until I knew what it was like to live so fancy."

Sometimes new problems can arise with one's child's in-laws. A friend told me, "This was something you just don't think of. My in-laws got very jealous because my mother came to live with us. She saw the children every day, they were crazy about her. My in-laws rarely saw their other grandchildren. They travel a lot and don't live near us. But when they realized my mother was much closer to the children, they became quite hostile toward her! Who could anticipate something as crazy as that?"

At no time in our lives, whatever the circumstances, can we anticipate every possibility. Life has a way of surprising us much of the time. The only thing we can try to plan for is our capacity to remain flexible and open to new situations. When I first met the Brooklyn grandma, she was sure she was stuck for the rest of her life. She was hopeless and depressed. We talked for a long time and I tried to tell her she still had options, but she said, "You're young, you don't understand, I have no energy for changing." I asked her to do me a favor—keep in touch, let me know how she was doing. A few months later I got a postcard from her. She wrote, "My Dear Mrs. LeShan: You are wise for your age! My son arranged for a car to take me back to my old neighborhood once a week. I see the butcher, the tailor, the children in my building, I have a wonderful Spanish lunch with my neighbors (I get heartburn but I don't mind!), and then a car picks me up. Last week I took my grandson with me so he should know there are good people everywhere."

Compromise, self-esteem on all sides, open communication are what are needed—but love most of all. When three generations live together out of love, all problems are surmountable.

❧ 13 ❧

When Grandparents Become Widowed, or Separate, Divorce, Remarry, or Choose a "Significant Other"

A FOUR-YEAR-OLD, very confused by the fact that Grandma and Grandpa had gotten a divorce and Grandma had a boyfriend, asked his mother, "If Grandma goes to a party, who will she dance with?" It is sheer pain and anxiety when parents divorce, but new life arrangements for grandparents can seem totally weird and perplexing. If anything in life is supposed to be steady, secure, and unchanging, it is the way in which grandparents behave.

Whatever the age of the child, grandparents need to be prepared to explain what is happening and to provide reassurance that the grandchild-grandparent relationship will continue to be as strong as ever.

A grandfather says, "Marjorie and I had many problems in our marriage, but we stayed together for our children—and then we didn't want to upset our grandchildren. But finally we felt we should have the freedom to separate and make new choices.

The biggest problem was that our grandchildren wanted to know who was the "good" grandparent and who was the "bad" one. They loved us both and they simply could not fathom the idea that we might both agree on the separation."

The issue of divorce in the later years is a subject unto itself, with many profound implications, challenges, and problems. That's another book! What I am concerned with here is how divorce and separation in the later years impact on grandchildren. There are special hazards for them in this situation: grandparents fighting, asking children and grandchildren to take sides; not making adequate plans for health and aging issues, such as including in the separation a full awareness of the increasing vulnerability of both partners. In a relatively young divorce, no matter how complex and difficult, it is more likely to be possible for both people to find solutions to such issues as housing, health care, and other necessities of life. These matters become even more crucial for older couples.

For the sake of grandchildren especially, plans need to be made carefully; bitterness and accusations ought to be a private matter. The children will need explanations of why this is happening and when and what the future will be like. A grandmother who was deserted suddenly by her husband was shocked, furious, and in great pain but managed to handle her grief with the help of friends and a divorce counselor. What she said to her grandchildren was, "I think Grandpa has been hurting in his feelings for quite a while. Some men get very, very upset about getting older and they decide they need to try to have more fun. Grandpa needs to know you will still love him and he certainly still loves you." Such a response is surely very difficult, but it shows the kind of courage and sensitivity that can lighten the anger and confusion of the children. They need to feel there will be a continuing relationship no matter what is happening. Before a final decision is made, grandparents ought to try to agree on what they are going to say to the grandchildren, how they are going to answer questions in a way that will be least damaging to their continuing role as grandparents. Blaming each other, dividing the grandchildren's loyalties, and asking them to take sides are surely not ways to preserve a secure relationship with the grandchildren.

This doesn't mean outright lying. While each grandparent may feel rejected, outraged, exploited, and deeply disillusioned, those are not feelings that children need to share. They can be told that there are irreconcilable problems and difficulties, that the couple have worked hard to solve their problems, that they want to go on respecting each other and caring what happens to the other person. Hopefully there may have been a period of counseling; it is productive for children to know that when there are serious problems grandparents can seek expert help and advice. It may also be helpful to say that when there is such a crisis, feelings may be too strong for a while for grandparents to see the children together, but a time will come when they will be able to forgive, understand, and maintain some kind of civilized relationship. When told his grandparents were separating, one teenager, obviously very upset, asked, "But, but, does that mean you won't both come to my graduation?" Hopefully the answer will be yes, even if Grandma and Grandpa don't sit together.

One of the most difficult issues is asking grandchildren to welcome a new person too soon. If a grandparent is in a new relationship, it may be helpful to the children not to be expected to accept this quickly. The new "significant other" had best not be invited to that important graduation. Children need time to heal. New relationships need to develop slowly, especially if, for example, there is a very dramatic difference in ages. A grandmother comments, "My two grandsons, seven and ten, were shocked that their grandfather's girlfriend was twenty years younger than he. The older child said to me, 'Grandma, I think you are still beautiful'! I was so touched, and it was hard not to say, 'Your grandfather is an old fool'—but I didn't! I told him not to worry about me—I felt good about myself. Of course, I cried all the way driving home!"

It is a difficult balance to be truthful but not to burden children with having to choose sides.

As in a divorce between a child's parents, what can make a serious situation devastating is if grandparents don't talk openly and honestly about what is happening. Betty devoted her life to taking care of her husband, who had had a serious stroke; he died ten years later, when Betty was fifty-five. A few years later Betty met Henry, widowed when his wife had a heart attack. At that time he was sixty-five. When Betty and Henry met, each had an apartment in the same senior community of retirees. Each wanted to go on living alone but sharing their lives. Each had a number of children and many grandchildren. They spent most of their time together—exercises in the morning, most meals together, watching television, going to movies, and then traveling together. They were in love but too embarrassed to let others know—they put on an act of just being good friends. Henry went to see his family, Betty went to see hers. There was little time spent with each other's families, and there was considerable formality when they did. On one Thanksgiving, when they went separately to their own celebrations, a teenage granddaughter at Betty's daughter's house announced loudly as the turkey was being carved, "For heaven's sake, Nana, we all know Henry is your boyfriend! Why can't you take turns on Thanksgiving, one year to his family and one year to ours?" Grandma almost went into cardiac arrest at this public announcement. Later she told me, "How stupid can you get? The little kids just took us for granted as a team, and the older children had known all along exactly what was going on!"

By keeping silent about changes in our lives we make two mistakes. The first is that we underestimate the grandchildren. I read recently about a grandchild who had been warm and loving but suddenly became distant and angry toward her grandmother. After much probing and questioning, she tearfully said, "I know Grandma and PopPop don't love each other anymore!" Neither grandparent had said anything about an impending separation, and this grandchild, who adored her grandfather, figured it must be Grandma's fault.

The same things need to be said that ought to be part of any parental divorce: The children are in no way responsible; nothing could happen that could lessen the love for the children, who will always be cherished; sometimes even people as old as grandparents can fall out of love and need to separate. Once their children are grown and have children of their own, grandparents who may not have been too happy want to try new adventures, do things that perhaps they have never done before. People who loved each other very much can change after being married for many, many years.

Grandparents who are separating need to talk to their adult children very seriously about helping the grandchildren. One grandmother told me, "My daughter has always clung to us—she is immature in many ways. When Dad and I told her we wanted to live apart, Sara carried on like a raving maniac, screaming, crying, making all kinds of accusations; we were going to ruin her life. We had a difficult relationship with her when she was growing up—I guess there was a lot of unfinished business, but now we had to be very firm with her; she was making our grandchildren feel we were rejecting her and them and that this event would change everything."

When we want to change our lives, it is amazing the "stuff" that comes out of the woodwork! Old rivalries between sons and daughters, anger at whatever failings children have been harboring about their childhood experiences, differences they perceive in our feelings about each child. We need to make it clear that displays of terror and anger will be hurtful to the grandchildren and are not to be tolerated. Quiet conversations when grandchildren are not present will be necessary.

Grandparents who feel they must make dramatic changes in their lives are more than likely to feel guilty! Quite natural in terms of the way in which we were raised—a much more sacrificial attitude when we were young—we are the generation that was supposed to be good to everyone but ourselves, so we have to work hard at not being overwhelmed by doubts and misgivings when we know we are doing what we need to do.

I had a friend who was a wonderful educator. She was the director of one of the most prestigious colleges focused on child development, a warm, loving, and brilliant woman. Her husband, who had never had a "calling" in the same way as his wife, retired from a dress-manufacturing business when his wife was at the height of her career. He wanted her to retire with him; he told her it was possible now to spend more time with the grandchildren. At first Laura refused, but then she gave in when she realized she was hurting her husband. She left her job—the joy of her life—and moved into a country house, big enough to accommodate all the grandchildren. The grandchildren were delighted; they had been afraid Grandpa would move to the country by himself. A year later they had no grandmother, who died of cancer; I believe giving up her special, wonderful life lowered her immune system until she got sick.*

The worst thing any human being can do to himself or herself is not to be true to one's unique needs, talents, and interests.

*See Lawrence LeShan, Ph.D., *Cancer as a Turning Point* (New York: New American Library, 1990).

That doesn't mean being cruel or unfeeling to others. All through life we make some concessions to others whom we love, but hopefully never giving up what is most essential to our own well-being. When the sacrifice is too great, and beyond what we should do to ourselves, we become very poor role models for our grandchildren. What we surely want for them is that they realize their own unique and important potentials; if we don't do it, how can they learn this essential human value?

One daughter-in-law told me, "Jake and I were stunned when his parents announced they were separating; we really had no idea. At first I was even more upset than Jake, and I couldn't figure out why. Later I realized I was jealous! I wanted to go back to work, maybe even get an advanced degree, but I felt guilty about the time I would be away from Jake and the kids. I went to see a shrink, who got the pitch in the first twenty minutes! My in-laws inspired me to fight for myself!"

Divorce may well follow many years of a pathological relationship; the ability finally to get out of a bad marriage takes great courage. It is never too late to assert one's right to dignity, self-respect, even safety from harm. But unless one partner has fallen in love with someone else and wants to make the total commitment to a new life, what seems to be happening is that many of the people in our generation, who had fits when our children began to have relationships outside of marriage, have discovered that it's not such a bad idea—and is not immoral if the people involved care about each other and are not exploiting each other or hurting anyone. Sometimes our grown children may object, but the grandchildren are likely to be very tolerant. We have discovered that maybe the "sixties kids" had something! People can respect and care for each other, take responsibility, without having a marriage license. Many women have told me that they have discovered living alone can be a blessing—nobody to take care of all the time. Most want to "have a relationship," a companion to have dinner with, to travel with, to share all kinds of recreational activities with—and even sex! When one seven-year-old asked his grandmother why "Uncle Eddy" was her boyfriend, she answered, "Since Grandpa died the only people who hug me are you and Dana, and your mom and dad and Aunt Frances; but lots of the time I'm alone and I like to have somebody nearby to hug me!" Who understands better about the need for hugs than little children?

My mother-in-law, widowed twice, never before having really been romantically in love, had a romance in her seventies and eighties. She was embarrassed, shy, fearful of being "found out." After Larry had given her the old "Go, girl, go!," her grandchildren were all ecstatic, admiring, respectful, and delighted. Not only did she allow herself a new life, but also she had a better relationship with her grandchildren than she'd ever had before. She had made the grade as a "hip grandma"!

When children don't seem to understand or like what may be happening and all efforts at reassurance have failed, it seems to me quite appropriate to set some limits: "I know you feel bad and I am sorry you are angry or sad, but I am a grown-up person and I have to decide what to do. I hope you will try to trust me and wish me the happiness that I always wish for you."

It may be necessary to make progress slowly. If there is a divorce and a remarriage, younger children may soon be ready to meet a new stepgrandparent by sharing a trip to the zoo or the carousel in the park with older grandchildren. The new spouse might just shake hands for a while but not try to be more demonstrative. Seeing each grandchild alone, for some special activity he or she loves too much not to go along, may be a way to break the ice. A new stepgrandparent told me, "Thank God I had season tickets to Yankee Stadium. It got us through the awkwardness and shyness."

There will be occasions when grandchildren will have a very

hard time adjusting to the change. This is especially true if they have already lived through their parents' divorce. Is anything secure or safe in their universe? If there are severe emotional stresses in their own family life and grandparents have represented an island of comfort and security, it may seem unbearable to live through this disruption. What is needed is infinite patience, no pressure, continual expressions of understanding and encouragement to express genuine, honest feelings.

A grandfather reported that his only grandson refused to see him after the separation. Grandpa was seeing a younger woman, a fact his grandson could not accept. Harry said, "I was devastated; he didn't understand all the facts, and I couldn't tell him. My wife had had a hysterectomy, was no longer interested in any sex life, and at seventy I was still sexually active. I tried everything—special outings, baseball games—he didn't want to see me at all. I decided to take the bull by the horns. I went over to my daughter's house after three o'clock, when I knew Bob would be home alone. He tried running into his room and slamming the door. I followed him. I told him how much I loved him, that I couldn't spend the rest of my life without him, and he should tell me exactly how he felt instead of not talking to me. He burst into tears, called me some terrible names, accused me of every sin you can imagine, and I took it without a word. After a while, it seemed all emotion was spent; we were both exhausted. I said I hoped someday he would understand and forgive me, but no matter how angry he was now, I thought we should see each other; we loved each other too much. He started crying again, came over and hugged me, we both cried, and now he seems to be able to see me and talk to me. I am prepared to wait as long as it takes, but meanwhile the air has been cleared."

It is harder to rework relationships if families live far apart. One grandmother told me, "It's expensive to travel, so we weren't getting together more than once a year. But I realized that whatever the sacrifice, both my ex-husband and I each had to visit more often for a while or we would drift apart forever. We had to establish the fact we would both be available, that we would go on loving the children. We each had to cash in some bonds, but it is one of those expenses you can't avoid. If we were sick we might have to do that; this was just as important."

One grandmother asked her twelve-year-old granddaughter if she was feeling better about her grandparents' divorce several years earlier. Both grandparents had remarried. Shelley said, "At first I felt awful, but after a while I realized I had two extra grandparents to love me—and I'd get presents from six grandparents at Christmas!"

Reconciliation happens; it just takes time, and we need to make it clear what we have done was right for us—inevitable and necessary. Respecting our needs even when we are getting old is a way of expressing an important message to grandchildren. Things happen—unexpected, frightening things—but love goes on.

❦14❧

Growing Old

SOME PEOPLE ARE not exactly overjoyed about becoming grandparents; it means only one thing to them: getting old. A friend told me she remembers that when she was about nine her grandmother whispered to her when they were going to an affair at Grandma's church, "Don't call me 'Grandma,' call me 'Aunt Judith.'" My friend was puzzled at the time, but when she told her mother about it her mother explained, "Grandma feels terrible about getting old. That's why she dyes her hair and dresses like a teenager and has facials every week. She made the people in the beauty parlor cover the mirrors with sheets one time when all the dye had to be washed out of her hair and her gray hair would be visible for a few minutes."

Who wants to get old? It sets an unavoidable timetable on our lives. Although we may feel healthy and able to lead active lives, we know contemporaries who are beset by aging problems: arthritis, heart attacks, strokes, digestive disorders, and so on.

Once when I was about sixty I found myself alone in a country house during a snowstorm. When I started to shovel the driveway, a new neighbor plowed through the snow, shouting, "You mustn't do that! I'll do it for you. It's dangerous for you!" At first I couldn't figure out what she was talking about and was shocked when I realized she considered me an old woman. After she left and after I had thanked her effusively, I went to look in the bathroom mirror. She was right: the wrinkles on my face made a perfect tick-tack-toe game. It was the first time I noticed. Ever since, I find myself watching as the wrinkles become more pronounced. I never thought I would be older than I felt—perhaps thirty-five or forty! Aging is a shock; rationally we know it has to happen; emotionally most of us reject the whole idea as being some kind of cruel mistake.

When young couples started a family in their early twenties (our generation included), grandparents could easily be in their forties. Now that so many of our children's generation have delayed parenthood until their thirties, even their forties, we are likely to be long in the tooth when we become grandparents. Some of us were very impatient with the delay: We felt betrayed, our own parents were still young enough to have a lot of fun with grandchildren—we may get more tired, even crotchety around noisy, demanding little kids. Many of us remember that when we had children our parents were relatively young, active, middle-aged. Becoming grandparents at a later age is both a relief that it has finally happened, and joy, as well as some concern about our capacity to handle the role.

One not very tactful grandson of seven, wiping dinner dishes with his grandmother, looked at her thoughtfully and said, "Grandma, you're getting so old—who will help me with the dishes when you're dead?" The specter of dying becomes more real with getting older, especially if we *are* older than we expected to be when grandchildren arrived.

A number of unexpected events have taken place in our lives—things we never anticipated, things that didn't usually happen to our parents when they were getting older. We are a "sandwich generation," caught between the needs of our children and grandchildren, and the needs of our own elderly parents, who are living so much longer (on the average) than any previous generation. There are times when it blows my mind that in my seventies I still have a parent who needs financial assistance and constant care. *I* am old, I say to myself; how come someone is older than I?

We are the generation that went to all the romantic movies of the thirties and forties. We expected rose-covered picket fences outside a charming cottage, or evening clothes worn all the time in penthouses. People over sixty had gray hair, walked with canes, looked one hundred and five, and died conveniently. In our sixties we are more than likely to be making the mortgage and car payments for our children in an awful economy; with most of our daughters working, we are frequently expected to be available for child care. Because we live longer and feel better, we work hard at being attractive and healthy, playing golf and tennis, fearful of retiring because so many people— the younger generation and the older generation—need our help. The mythical movie picture of our slowly walking toward the sunset with a loving mate, or on the way to Florida or a world cruise, seems to have been postponed for many of us.

Of course, we all know people who are having a perfectly fine old time. A warm, loving cousin of mine, who has always been crazy about little kids, baby-sits for her daughter-in-law two full days a week and couldn't be happier. She became a grandmother at fifty-three. There are retirement communities all over the country, so it is clear a great many people have found ways of enjoying their lives as they grow old. But the amount of serious depression, even suicide, among the elderly suggests all is not well. Many mourn for their youth, for the things they did that they can't do anymore; widowhood brings grief and mourning. Every day I am reminded, unhappily, that my upper teeth are not my own and that my arthritic knees have removed one of my great pleasures, bicycling on country roads. Our savings are diminishing—we worry about chronic illnesses. A financial manager told Larry we must save for a rainy day. He replied, "It's already *pouring*!"

Social changes have given us more choices, but at the same time the population has grown so much that we fear the time when we may not have the resources to help ourselves; Social Security was a humane invention, but what if that's all we've got if we get sick? And what if it is taken away? We worry plenty, but fortunately there are moments of exhilaration, too, when we are witness to a wonderful spirit, when we see an urge not only to survive as well as possible, but perhaps to live more fully than ever. Whenever I feel down I think about Larry's Aunt Ida. At eighty, living in a nursing home, she met Sam, aged eighty-four, who had a serious heart condition. They fell in love, and because the nursing home made no effort to accommodate their passion, they very cleverly discovered they could stop the elevator between floors to kiss, hug, and talk. They were both dead a year later, but Ida had had the love of her life.

I have a friend who started law school at age fifty-seven and at eighty-three is a volunteer advocate for poor people in trouble who can't pay a lawyer. All of us know people who should be our role models. They are not necessarily those rare creatures who have the genetic good luck never to feel sick. A neighbor had two hip replacements that didn't mend properly, and for the rest of her life she will be in a wheelchair. As a former school teacher, she called the principal of a neighborhood school and offered to tutor some of the children with learning problems, in her home. The kids adore her; when one of them graduated from high school he insisted that he would do her shopping for her once a week while working to earn money for college.

It seems to me that one of the most important functions of grandparents is to be role models. Unless people from another planet appear and tell us about a magical drug that will keep us forever young, our children and grandchildren are someday going to be old. The best people to help children accept the ages and stages of life with some grace and a lot of courage are us. If we deal with our adversities, our disappointments, and our frustrations creatively, we will leave an indelible impression on our grandchildren.

One grieving grandmother, whose husband had died after a long illness, was asked by her teenage granddaughter, "Nana, how do you go on living when you and PopPop loved each other so much?" Grandma answered, "Sooner or later we have to face being widowed if we live longer than our partner. PopPop and I talked about it. We promised each other we would keep doing the things that had been important to both of us. When PopPop got sick, he told me that you and my other grand-children needed me; he wanted me to tell you about his early life, to give you our honeymoon pictures. He wanted me to save some of the things he loved the most to give to you when you grew up—paintings, books—even his pipes. Even though I am sad and I miss him so much, I need to go on living for his sake and mine, so you can remember who we are and how much we love you."

A middle-aged mother with two sons in college wrote me:

> I read your columns and I think you would appreciate hearing this story. My father is dying of cancer; he has been through horrendous treatments with awful side effects. He's in pain all the time, no matter how much morphine they give him. Once a robust, healthy, active person, he is shriveling before my eyes.

He's lost sixty pounds, he has no hair. But he wears a jaunty baseball cap, and when my sons visit him he makes the most heroic efforts to speak to them, to tell them how he loves them, how he has enjoyed being their grandfather. Both boys were weeping in the hospital hall the last time they came to see him, and when I tried to comfort them my older son told me I didn't understand—they were not crying because he would soon die, but because for the rest of their lives they would never forget this most wonderful man they had ever known.

There are many periods in our lives that call for ingenuity, patience, bravery. At no time is this more true than in the last quarter of our lives. Sometimes it seems as if it would be easy to give up. But it is a time when what is best and most profoundly human about us can give meaning to our lives and leave a legacy of marvelous memories. Instead of focusing our attention on the discomforts, frustrations, and anxieties that may be perfectly normal and appropriate to our time of life, we need to think about the legacy we will leave for our grandchildren. Will they remember that we complained endlessly about the things we could no longer do, or will they remember how we tried to do everything it was still possible for us to do? Will they remember that we told them, "Never get old—it's too horrible," or will they remember that we told them we loved life and wanted to live every minute of it as fully as possible?

A friend of ours was dying of an advanced, incurable cancer. Larry has worked for more than forty years with cancer patients, trying through psychotherapy to help people come to the aid of the immune system through insight, new adventures, and a sense of self-worth. Adam wanted Larry to work with him, although the doctors had told him he couldn't live more than three months. His daughter was sitting with him in the hospital and asked, "Daddy, what's the use of working with Larry?" Adam replied, "Everybody dies sooner or later. What Larry is helping me do is to die with *style*." His daughter and grandchildren know that Grandpa fought for his life—even got well enough to travel, to paint, to write letters to all his loved ones about his life, his feelings. Grandparents can teach moral values, and never more effectively than when they are dying. Their grandchildren need to be helped to see that death is a reality we cannot deny but that it teaches us that life is so precious we ought not waste a moment of it. What that means is fulfilling our own dreams, perhaps doing things we never had time for before—or gave up for some more immediate goals or responsibilities. One four-year-old was stroking his grandmother's face. He said, "Your skin is very old and soft. I guess you will die soon." Grandma answered, "I will die someday, but meanwhile I am much too busy watching you grow up and enjoying your kisses and hugs."

Many grandchildren find it almost impossible to understand what it is like to be getting old. We sense a genuine generation gap and may find this hard to deal with. Some children and grandchildren need to deny that we are getting older—they are too frightened of our leaving them. I have a neighbor who is seventy-seven. She gets out of breath very often, has palpitations, gets dizzy if she moves too suddenly. One day, when her granddaughter called and found Betty still in bed at 11:00 A.M., she told her, "Grandma, you're just not getting enough exercise! That's your whole problem. You must go for a walk every day. Start with an hour and gradually increase it." My neighbor and I had a good laugh. We agreed that we hoped her granddaughter would remember this conversation when *she* was seventy-seven.

One of my regrets is how little I understood my mother. It annoyed me when she insisted she had to stand in line to go to the bathroom before we saw a play; when I barbecued a delicious steak and she said she was sorry she couldn't chew it, I was angry. When she seemed to spend a great deal of time focused on the problems of her lower colon I decided she had

a neurotic fixation. Now that I am suffering all the same in-
dignities, how I wish I could apologize!

A friend of mine has a very rambunctious two-year-old granddaughter. She told her daughter that she'd love to baby-sit for
one or two hours, but it was just too exhausting for her to baby-
sit all day. Her daughter replied, "I just *knew* you didn't want
me to have a third child, so now you're punishing me!" How I
wish I could live long enough to see how this cruel and unfeeling daughter manages to baby-sit when *she's* seventy-six!

When I was in my early forties, there was an education conference I attended every year. A group of us became close
friends, and after a day's meeting we would go off to a nearby
tavern, eat pizzas, drink a few beers, laugh, sing, and have a
wonderful time. There was one member of our group who was
in her midsixties, and while she often went along with us,
protesting it was long past her bedtime, she would have some
tea and toast. Stupid me would tease her: Why wasn't she more
adventurous, why didn't she "follow the pleasure principle" like
the rest of us?

Sarah looked me straight in the eye and solemnly said, "Eda,
I want you to remember this night when you are sixty. I want
you to remember that I couldn't eat pizza at midnight and still
go to sleep."

I should have been on the tea-and-toast routine by the time
I was fifty, and I have never forgotten Sarah. Unfortunately, I am
a less disciplined person and have my share of sleepless nights.

Most of the intolerance of older people seems to have to do
with our physical infirmities, which younger people simply cannot comprehend, but there is another generation gap that drives
me nuts and that is the inference that age has made us stupid!

People half my age often give me advice, warnings, and suggestions that might be appropriate for nursery-age children. We
must constantly remind ourselves that even though we may
think more slowly, or experience memory problems, these are

outweighed and are corrected by our maturity, our life experiences.

We may only be able to walk a half mile—slowly; we may have to think longer and more carefully in planning a day's activities. I forget words and names at least ten times a day. I search frantically for my glasses when they are hanging around my neck. But age need not be destiny. We can still use what we've got creatively and joyfully. And it would be a very good idea to encourage younger people to try to understand the aging process. They will be there eventually themselves. Even that niece, an enthusiastic jogger, may someday be glad to walk half a mile—slowly.

A friend is seventy-four; she has high blood pressure, tires easily, and is in a state of battle fatigue, having worked like a plow horse to raise three children, alone. She is *tired*. In a telephone conversation with her son she mentioned that some friends in a distant state where coming to New York and wondered if they could stay with her overnight. My friend felt overwhelmed at the thought, but her son said, "Ma, why are you making such a fuss? Just throw two chickens in the oven!"

I suspect no one under sixty could understand that this was advice that could only fuel the fire of anger and misunderstanding. We could, at one time, not only have thrown the chickens in the oven, but we probably would have baked some pies, arranged a dinner party with mutual friends, given the guest room a thorough cleaning, and planned to make eggs Benedict for breakfast. I remember how angry and mystified I was when my mother, in her sixties and early seventies, "made a fuss" about having company, even for afternoon tea. How I wish I could apologize now! *Something happens* as we get older, and one of the somethings is the loss of the capacity to handle things that we once could do with both eyes shut and at least one hand tied behind our back.

On a four-day visit several years ago to our daughter, son-in-

law, and granddaughter, we drove five and a half hours, sat on a narrow wooden bench watching a two-hour horseback-riding lesson, sat on a damp stone (muddy) wall at a campfire, went swimming in the rain, played a long game of Monopoly, ate too much, and stayed up too late at a dinner party in our honor. All lovely things to have done—at fifty. But at sixty-eight and seventy it meant going to bed for a day when we got home.

It is hard to tell our adult children that we are *really* getting old. If they love us, that frightens them—we are mentioning mortality. But there are things we can do. I told my grand-daughter that once upon a time I could ride a bicycle ten miles a day and I'm sorry she couldn't have seen me run up a flight of stairs, but I can do other things, such as write children's books and dedicate them to her. And my husband and I decided a five-hour trip must now be done in two days instead of one. We must try to be gentle with the news, but insist that our increasing infirmities are acknowledged.

It's a serious problem. Every time I have to tell my grand-daughter that I'm too tired to run to catch a ball or read a seventh story, I feel guilty about making her see me as old. I don't want her to worry. I know there are grandparents who remain a match not only for grandchildren but also for tennis and jogging at ninety, but my personal research strongly suggests that this is a lucky minority. My friends and I bring each other chicken soup after a visit from the grandchildren.

There is one pretty universal characteristic about the aging process: We tend to become very nostalgic about the past; everything was easier, cleaner, quieter, better when we were young; no traffic problems, no mobs of shoppers, people were more polite to each other—on and on with clouded memories! This annoys younger generations; they get tired of hearing how great life used to be, and if we are reasonably honest it behooves us to acknowledge that we can get places faster by flying and we can be cured more quickly of what ails us, and despite the explosions of hatred between whites and blacks, more people share their lives, neighborhoods, schools, and jobs than ever before. We have a right to happy memories, but we need to remember that a rosy glow sometimes distorts the reality. We need to find a balance between the importance and pleasure for both young and old in sharing history, but we need to make an effort to accept that each period of our lives—past, present, future—has positive and negative aspects, and we need to watch for that glazed look that comes to the faces of our audience when we overdo a good thing. The present and the future remain more important than the past.

I know I have to help the younger members of my family understand my limitations, but I am far more concerned about showing them what I can still do. I am about to tell a story that those of you who have heard me speak or have read my books already know; if you know my "Lobster Story," you can now skip it. But it's too important to leave out.

At a dinner party many years ago, I sat next to a man who was an oceanographer. He turned out to be a fascinating man. At one point he asked me if I had ever wondered why lobsters could weigh one pound, three pounds, even ten pounds when they had such a hard shell—how could they grow? I had to tell him this was a problem that was not very high on my list of priorities. He smiled and proceeded to tell me that when a lobster becomes crowded in its shell and can't grow anymore, by instinct it travels out to some place in the sea, hoping for relative safety, and begins to shed its shell. It is a terribly dangerous process—the lobster has to risk its life, because once it becomes naked, vulnerable, it can be dashed against a reef or eaten by another lobster or fish. But that is the only way it can grow. The pink membrane under the shell begins to harden in the salt water, and the new shell will be bigger, roomier. When that shell gets too tight the whole process will have to take place all over again.

I was preoccupied with this story—I even began dreaming about lobsters! Finally I mentioned it to my therapist—why was I so absorbed in this story? She was a very smart lady. She said, "Eda, it's perfectly clear: You're writing a book about the crisis of middle age, and lobstering is what it's all about."

Since that time Larry and I have known when it was time to "go to the reef," when it was time to grow and change, to become more than we have been. It is frightening, but we both have a divine discontent: We want more and more out of life. Staying in a tight shell is a metaphor for stagnation.

Right now, as I write this, I am having panic attacks at night; I am terrified, but I have become too imprisoned in my present shell—a very comfortable one. I could live easily where I am; I have an office overlooking the Hudson River and the Palisades, a happy marriage, a decent income if we don't become too extravagant. For several years I have had a growing feeling that I need something new and different at this point in my life; I need to leave New York and live in the country; I need to watch birds at feeders and splashing in a fountain. I need a cat (an indoor one!), and I need to talk to ducks. I need to walk in the woods. But most of all, I need to have the courage to do something I have wanted to do all my life but never had the courage to do—write plays, even do some acting.

We are going to face possible bankruptcy—we have no guarantee we can sell my office apartment at a time of a serious recession, but while visiting my daughter on Cape Cod I found the house of my dreams. If I searched for ten more years I couldn't match it: a private beach, a yacht club where my granddaughter can go to a sailing camp, a short walk to stores, wooded paths for walking—and an amateur theater group where there is a director who has heard of me and says I can get workshop productions of any plays I write. I lie awake in a cold sweat, terrified to use up so much of our hard-earned bulwark against poverty in old age, but I have to "go to the reef" at least this one more time. I will be near my eleven-year-old granddaughter; we have never had enough time together. She is so proud and happy about what her grandparents are doing that her teacher told my daughter she wanted to meet Rhiannon's grandparents, since she was so overjoyed they were taking this big chance. She told Wendy, "I've never *seen* such excitement about grandparents moving nearby."

I recommend to other grandparents that we keep our lives exciting, that we challenge ourselves, even when we may be scared to death. We have to teach our grandchildren that dying is not a sin; not living fully is.

❧ 15 ❧

When Therapy Can Help

MANY YEARS AGO, when I was working in a child guidance clinic, I had a nine-year-old patient who became very disturbed (school phobia, fear of the dark, etc.) after witnessing a child being run over by a car in front of his school. We saw each other once a week for an hour for about six months. We played games and talked, often about accidents and death, about aggressive and hostile feelings, about how we can love and hate at the same time. At the last session, while we were saying good-bye to each other, Michael said, "When I came here my heart was hurting. It doesn't hurt so much anymore." I have never heard a better description of psychotherapy.

Life is full of painful, frightening experiences, and often, when they occur, they bring to consciousness old wounds. In Michael's case, when he witnessed the accident he was reminded of his own earlier experiences and especially his ambivalent feelings toward his mother. She was a strong, aggressive, sometimes overpowering woman, and when the accident occurred,

Michael probably felt (unconsciously) that there were times when he had been angry and frustrated and would have been happy to run his mother over. He also loved her and was terrified that his "bad thoughts" might make something bad happen to her. During the third month of our being together, Michael took a toy truck and a small wooden doll and had the truck run over the doll while he joyfully sang a song popular at that time, "I Don't Want Her, You Can Have Her, She's Too Fat for Me!"

You can believe I found this perfect grist for my psychological mill! We talked at length about the absolute difference between *thinking* something and *doing* something. Everybody has angry thoughts, which are normal and okay. But that doesn't mean we will hurt the person at whom we are angry.

When "bad things happen to good people" I don't ask why, but rather what we can do about it.

All the therapists at the clinic had predicted that some children would come to the clinic after the accident. The ones who became most troubled would be those, like Michael, with a hidden agenda.

I have already described in this book so many of the complexities in human relationships that it is no wonder at all that many people need professional help with their problems. How lucky we are that it's now available.

A grandparent wrote me, "I wish you could explain to me why my daughter and son-in-law and their child are seeing a therapist. In the first place, I feel guilty: Did I do something wrong to my daughter? And in the second place, my grandson isn't sick; he has some trouble learning, and sometimes he seems overexcited. I admit he has a temper, but is that a reason for a shrink? If everyone with a temper had to go to a head doctor, there would be long lines around every office."

What a lucky grandma! Too bad she doesn't know it. When she was young, people died of peritonitis because there wasn't any penicillin. People also suffered from psychological problems because nobody understood them or knew what to do about them. Now no child need die of a burst appendix, and hopefully more and more children will be helped with their unhappy feelings early enough so they can fulfill their potentials and feel worthwhile and self-confident when they grow up.

I feel sad that my mother felt so challenged, frightened, and guilty the first time I went to see a therapist. What had she done wrong? I wish I had been able to help her see it was what she had done *right* that made me want to examine my share of hangups, made me want to grow, to live more fully. How I wish *she* could have had the kind of help I was getting, when at four her mother died and like any four-year-old she figured it must have been her fault. She lived for seventy-eight years with a terrible inner wound.

Never once, in more than forty years in the field of child psychology, did I ever come across *anybody* who wasn't carrying some evidence of crippling experiences in childhood—some serious, some less so. Because it takes so long for children to gain a sense of perspective about events around them, they misunderstand, they blame themselves for everything that goes wrong. It never occurs to a young child that a parent or teacher or grandparent could ever be wrong; obviously if only the child was good, bad things would never happen. Every child ever born bears some of this burden of confusion and misunderstanding. More of today's parents are trying to make it clear to children that they are not responsible for family disasters of any kind; and when children seem to be overwhelmed by inner obstacles, parents want to prevent future unhappiness by solving the problems as early as possible.

Psychotherapy, when it's good (and a therapist must be chosen with as great care and research as a surgeon or a lawyer), is simply a way of clearing up confusion and encouraging a sense of self-worth; it is an avenue toward growing and changing, which should be everyone's life tasks.

Grandma has nothing to feel guilty about. She's just terribly lucky that her daughter and son-in-law are using the emotional penicillin now available to us.

Sigmund Freud said, "At some time during therapy the therapist loves the patient, and the patient knows it. And the healing begins." This is a very profound statement about how therapy heals. All of us are crippled to some extent by misunderstandings between parent and child, and most of us have a sense of doubt about our worthiness as human beings. Lack of confidence, lack of a positive image of ourselves, tends to make it harder for us to move toward the fullest possible self-realization.

Larry and I have used psychotherapy as a tool for growing and changing. We have never felt fully content with ourselves—we have always felt there was more we could be and become. We could have settled for what we were at any given time during our adulthood, but always felt there were powers, talents, insights ahead, just around the corner for us to explore. It has been a wonderful adventure. I never have felt that seeking some sort of counseling was a sign of weakness, but rather of strength and courage. We have found that many life crises are lived through more creatively with the help of therapy. Marital problems, choices about careers, dealing with illness, becoming better parents seem to me to have been greatly facilitated by talking to someone who can see us more clearly than we can see ourselves.

When your children and grandchildren search for better answers to normal emotional problems, they are showing good sense and courage. There now is this new avenue for helping children avoid serious difficulties in adulthood.

When children are under age five or six I have very serious questions about their becoming involved in individual psychotherapy for one reason only: They are too young to judge the therapist. In any field of endeavor there are artists and drones; there are exceptionally sensitive human beings and many robotlike followers of one rigid theory. Young children have no criteria by which to measure whether they are being helped or damaged further.

Sitting in on a meeting at a mental health center, I had the privilege of listening to a great child psychiatrist, Anina Brandt. At one point a therapist asked her, "Dr. Brandt, what school of psychotherapy do you belong to?" Dr. Brandt looked absolutely blank and then, stuttering a little, she said, "But—but—how can I tell until I see the child?"

It is that philosophy that seems essential to me—that a therapist explore the heart and soul of each person as a unique individual. I also believe that helpful therapy is as concerned with all the wonderful qualities of a person as with the troubled side.

Your adult children will, of course, choose their own therapist. The more we know about psychology and psychiatry, the more we may be able to engage in some conversations about their choices, but never interfering unless something really awful seems to be happening. A grandmother told me that her daughter, Kathleen, had always been somewhat fragile emotionally. After the birth of her second child she went into postpartum depression and was referred to a therapist by her gynecologist. Her parents and her husband became aware of the fact that Kathleen was getting worse; they were terrified she might commit suicide. Grandpa had a friend who was a psychiatrist, and with his son-in-law's permission asked his friend to find out about the therapist. It turned out that his methods of treatment were extremely rigid and even hostile and that he was experimenting with various drugs. They found a family counselor who talked to Kathleen about the normal terrors and frustrations of parenthood and gave her sensible and practical advice about managing with two children close in age. What Kathleen actually got was a kind of intense mothering and nurturing from an impartial expert—what she needed.

In the past twenty-five or so years a new kind of therapy has emerged that can be very helpful: family therapy. In part it grew out of the fact that sometimes, when a child seems deeply troubled, when his behavior becomes frightening, unacceptable, the child is not always the person in the family who is most troubled. The child is a kind of "bell ringer," trying to draw attention to what is now called "a dysfunctional family." Family therapy can point to multiple family problems. Ordinarily every member of the family participates. In this case very young children can be involved; they need to know what is happening to the family—not to be left out, where they will imagine everything that's going wrong is their fault! Often grandparents are welcomed into the family group, but sometimes not, depending on the parents and the therapist. Being left out—perhaps for a while—does not mean that all that's wrong is their fault. It usually means that the family needs space and time for itself.

Like individual therapy, family therapy can be wonderful or terrible, depending on who's in charge. When everyone feels free to communicate genuine feelings with an expert who can use these feelings constructively, a family can learn successful techniques for dealing with its problems. It can be very helpful during a divorce, where both parents and children can express their anger, their sense of failure, their pain, and be helped to develop the strength and the skills for recovery from serious traumatic events.

Not always; a friend of mind called me to tell me of her experience with family therapy. She was asked to participate by her son and daughter-in-law along with the two grandchildren, girls of three and seven. Very quickly she realized she had been included because the family felt she was drinking too much. (She is not an alcoholic but enjoys several drinks each day.) She was attacked by her son for every hurt he had ever suffered as a child; her daughter-in-law said my friend interceded too much in discipline. The parents said they didn't trust

Grandma when she was alone with the children; she might drink too much. My friend said, "I have never been attacked that way in my life. My son blamed me for divorcing his father when Jerry was eight. Nothing about the fact that Ben was having multiple affairs! The therapist just let it go on and on, and I nearly died when I saw the shock in the eyes of my seven-year-old granddaughter. The younger child must have sensed what was happening to me and tried to crawl in my lap, but her mother told her to go and sit down in her own chair! Is this what family therapy is—a nightmare?"

Certainly not. There are excellent family therapists who may let a lot of things "hang out" but who are skilled in bringing about more positive and loving relationships and would never let a grandparent be attacked in front of grandchildren.

On the other hand, a widower grandfather told me, "I didn't want to have anything to do with sitting in on what I thought would just be a family fight. But I was fascinated; I learned so much about how my daughter and son-in-law were struggling to resolve their conflicts. I had so much new respect for them and learned ways in which I could help. It was one of the best learning experiences of my life!"

Family therapy at its best can bring out what is perhaps the most important function of grandparents—to support those who need it, to encourage, and to try to enhance the lives of children and grandchildren.

Many grandparents have asked me about providing financial help for psychotherapy. I can't think of any greater gift. I have also talked with many grandparents who are either terrified of the idea of getting therapy for themselves, or are eager to explore this avenue of enrichment but have no idea how to go about it.

I met a lawyer who, knowing I wrote about getting old, told me about his mother. He said, "My father died a year ago. They never got along well, there were constant fights all during my childhood. When he died, she acted as if she had lost not only the love of her life, but also her life. She won't do anything for herself, sits in her apartment, expects me and my wife to include her in everything we do, go shopping for her, take her to the doctor. We are going out of our minds." He asked me what he could do.

I suggested that they find a counselor or a group that dealt with widowhood. She could come to understand her mourning, begin to meet new people, move back into life among the living. This suggestion was greeted with fury. "Are you telling me I'm a crazy person? Is this how you help me with my terrible life? I wish I could drop dead right now!" This lawyer wasn't overjoyed with my advice!

The worse a marriage relationship may have been, the more painful may be the grief. It takes enormous energy to deal with denial—to avoid facing the fact of a failed relationship, to deal with what was wrong. I know one widower who has never touched his wife's clothes, still has her knitting and her glasses on the coffee table; she died several years ago. His daughter tells me, "They hated each other's guts! You could hear them screaming at each other two blocks away." Therapy can help such people deal with their real feelings and begin to have some compassion for themselves and their spouse; to accept their tragic circumstances and learn the possibilities for a new life.

Therapy can be helpful when grief and mourning occur in any of our lives. It's hard to move forward when we feel crushed, wounded, paralyzed by grief. Our generation has a new problem: parents who are living so long that our emotional and financial resources are being strained. Because so many people are living into their late nineties, even one hundred and older, we are faced with the problems of nursing homes, constant supervision and care for our parents, never enough financial resources, Alzheimer's disease and senility when we watch a beloved parent become strange, incontinent, demanding, well in body but disappearing in mind. It helps a great deal to meet with other people in similar circumstances, to have a chance to ventilate our feelings in a support group or individual counseling.

There are times when we know we mustn't interfere but are still deeply troubled about a child who seems hostile to us, a grandchild who is failing in school, an in-law who shouts constantly at our grandchild. We see that unless we keep our mouth shut, we will make things worse. Often seeing a therapist ourselves can help us understand what is going on and provide us with skillful ways of dealing with our concerns.

Choosing a therapist is very important. One has to go shopping, just as we do in choosing a friend or an employee. A person recommended by someone you realize has been helped may be the first person you see. Do you like the office, the paintings, the books on the shelves? Does this person greet you warmly, spontaneously, or do you feel he or she is being self-conscious and "properly professional"? Ask questions about the therapist's philosophy of life, his or her training, ideas about the goals of therapy. If the therapist says, "I am a Freudian [or Adlerian or Jungian, etc.]," I'd move cautiously. I have always chosen therapists who say, "Of course I have studied all the different theories, but I have to get to know the person and the problem and then we become companions in trying to deal with what is happening," or words to that effect. If you feel good about this person, try it out for two or three sessions. If you decide this isn't the right person for you, try someone else. If any therapist says, when you say you are not coming back, "Well, of course you are just resisting therapy," you will know you have made the right decision to leave!

Sometimes grandparents can see problems a parent hasn't noticed. Or the parent may be so busy raising a family and going to work so stressed out that he or she may not notice a problem. A grandparent may notice that Alexia looks sad too often, or Justin confides, "Grandma, I hate school; the teacher doesn't like me, and the other kids tease me." Some parents don't believe in psychotherapy—they say, "He'll grow out of it," or "She's just got a rotten personality." Or you notice that three years after a divorce the children seem emotionally torn apart in their loyalties. If you say, "I don't know what is the matter with you that you can't see this child needs help!" you might as well go home and forget about it. If you ask a few questions, offer comfort and support about how difficult life can be, and maybe help a little, you may be able to make the necessary suggestion. We need to remember, though, that what we may decide is a problem may not be serious enough so that something needs to be done. There are stages of growing up when children have temper tantrums, steal, fail in school, become totally noncommunicative, can't make friends, get pimples, hate themselves, and so on. These really are normal aspects of growing up. And they pass. We need to be cautious about turning normal problems into serious disturbances.

What seems important to me is that we become as well informed as we can about the "helping professions" and take our lead from our adult children. And most of all, we are not responsible, guilty, for every problem our adult children encounter. We did the best we could. We ought to be glad that they often have better information and resources than we may have had. What we ought to hope for them is that they will consider life a great adventure and will want to make the most of it.

When our daughter was about twenty, someone asked her what it was like being raised by two psychologists. Her answer was, "They made all the same mistakes other parents make, but I knew they were always trying to grow and change." That's what therapy—and life!—are all about.

❧ 16 ☙

That Very Special Kind of Love

IN AN ARTICLE in the March 4, 1983, *New York Times Sunday Magazine,* Russell Baker wrote, "It's nice being a grandchild. You're sitting on the floor being screamed at by Mommy for shaving the Oriental rug with Daddy's razor, and the phone rings, and it's Granddaddy saying, 'Bring that kid over here so I can love him up!' "

Russell Baker has this annoying habit of saying, in a few sentences, what I have needed a whole book to write about. It has happened before. Well, there it is; what it finally comes down to is grandparents are for unconditional love—meant to express the extraordinary and wonderful belief that there never were any children as adorable, brilliant, and beautiful as their own grandchildren.

This may well be what has thus far saved the human race from total, catastrophic self-destruction. In each of millions of crippled souls there may be just a glimmer of memory—once, long ago, someone thought we were perfect.

One grandmother went to a fancy, expensive supermarket for her daughter while she was in the hospital having another baby. Number one grandchild was with Grandma, who had rushed out of the house to do the food shopping. She happened to be wearing an apron and a kerchief on her head. The grocery clerk asked, "Are you the help?" Grandma replied, "Yes." Maybe that "help" is a little more complicated than unconditional love, although that is the source of all else.

I was a wonderfully lucky child. All four grandparents loved me to excess. But that wasn't the whole story. They were also beacons of light in teaching me what it meant to be an ethical, moral, caring person. Their passionate sense of *family* was a bulwark against all the normal terrors of life. I learned about the past from them; I came to understand the cycles of human life, from birth to death.

I became a parent during the years when many experts were saying grandparents were expendable; they were no longer the teachers, the advisers to young parents. Dr. Spock had taken over the job. Now raising children was becoming "scientific" and grandparents didn't know the new theories. Of course, Benjamin Spock, that dear, sweet, gentle man, must have thought these antigrandparent experts were nuts; I sure did. By the time I began to meet with parents to discuss "the new theories of childraising," I knew only too well that grandparents were special gifts.

I had a colicky baby who cried about twenty hours a day. I was terrified, awash in guilt; I must be doing something wrong. My mother came to Chicago to help. Within a day or two we were both basket cases. When my father heard what was going on he took a train to Chicago to relieve both of us. (Larry was away negotiating a vital army placement.) I think I might have murdered the baby and then killed myself if they hadn't come. Before anyone ever thought of the term for recovering alcoholics or cancer patients, grandparents were the original *sup-*

port group. My parents didn't always approve of later crises in Wendy's life, especially during the rebellious sixties, but never for a moment did they stop loving their granddaughter or stop offering help.

However, there is a fine line between doing everything possible to provide a grandchild with a strong feeling of self-worth and boasting about accomplishments that please us. For example, one grandfather says, "Kenny is going to be some baseball player! Takes after his grandfather already." It might be more comfortable for Kenny if he said, "I'm having such fun when we bat balls back and forth!"

If we boast to our friends, "Marie is a mathematical genius," or "Robbie got three A's and two B's on his report card," or "You should hear Aaron play that violin—I think he's going to be a child prodigy!," the children sense a demand, a level of perfection that becomes a heavy burden. Let parents and teachers deal with praise as well as demands and expectations. That is not a role for grandparents. We need to give our grandchildren a sense of high self-esteem just because they were born and we love them.

An important goal for grandparents is not to compete with parents. We need to search for a fine balance. One day, when my granddaughter was angry at her mom, my granddaughter said, "Grandma treats me better than you do!" I answered, "I don't have to raise you, help you learn and become a good citizen. Your parents have the hard part—they have to help you grow up every day. I have it easy—I just have to enjoy you."

You may by now be thoroughly bored by my constant theme of unconditional love as the main requirement of grandparents. I guess I think it's so important, that I overstate the case. There is a Puerto Rican saying that sums up the whole subject in a couple of sentences: "If someone boasts about himself, others say, 'I guess he has no grandmother—that's why he has to boast about himself!' "

Another essential role for grandparents is to serve as family historians. Larry tells wonderful animal stories that have been enjoyed by several generations of children. One time when I was alone with my granddaughter, she asked me to tell her a story at bedtime. I told her I just didn't have that talent, only her grandfather was very good at stories, but I could tell her real stories about my life and about her great-grandparents, and what life was like growing up many, many years ago. That suited her fine; Grandpa and I have separate jobs. Mine is to give Rhiannon a historical perspective. She was fascinated to know that her great-grandparents had no electric lights or cars or radios when they were young. I'm not sure she believed my weird statement that I grew up with no television! She loves to hear about the trolley car I rode to school. She thinks I'm joking when I tell her stamps cost three cents and subway rides were five cents when I was young. We are the historians of our families, bringing the past into their lives.

It is frequently our job to help a grandchild through the grief of the death of one grandparent. Often we will need to discuss openly, honestly, the change in a grandparent disabled by a stroke or something as terrifying as Alzheimer's disease; to make it clear that somewhere deep inside there is still the person who loved them. We need to let them know there are things to be sad and angry about. The tendency of my generation of parents was too often the idea that if you didn't acknowledge a feeling, it would go away, and that we could protect children from pain. Now we know, beyond a shadow of a doubt, that feelings can only change, get better, when expressed and dealt with.

At a time when my granddaughter was having a particularly hard time over the divorce of her parents and wasn't able to talk about her feelings, I told her the story of "Granjean" (my mother) and the dentist. When my mother was about five years old, she needed to go to the dentist. This was in about 1900, when dentistry was much more frightening than it is today. Her grandfather was taking her to the dentist and she was screaming and carrying on as he tried to pull her along the street. When they passed a fancy French bakery my mother said she'd be a good girl if her grandfather bought her a napoleon. He must have thought it was a reasonable bargain; my mother sat down on the curb, ate the napoleon, and suddenly stood up and ran home. Later her grandfather made her sit down in front of him. Then he lectured her on being such a bad girl. He said nobody could ever trust her and that she couldn't have any desserts for one month. He said he was very disappointed, and so would her father and all the rest of the family be.

My mother cried and cried. Her mother had died the year before, and like most four-year-olds my mother was sure it had been her fault. Now she was doubly sure she was a bad girl. She never forgot what her grandfather had said. When I finished the story, Rhiannon was quiet and thoughtful. Finally she said, "He should have been sorry for her. She was scared." I asked what the grandfather should have done. Rhiannon answered, "He should have said he understood she was scared and that a terrible thing had happened to her when her mother died and she wasn't bad, just sad and frightened."

I told Rhiannon she was absolutely right. And then Rhiannon said, "Like me." A family story had helped her begin to express feelings she now realized were universal.

Surely there are so many ways in which we can serve some special needs of our own grandchildren. But the word "grand-parent" ought to be a generic term. *All* children need uncon-ditional love, and there are millions of them who for one reason or another don't have grandparents or very rarely see them. I think we need to extend ourselves to participate in the lives of children who do not belong to us. There are churches in many parts of the country that have foster grandparent programs. Young families may live too far away to spend holidays with grandparents, for example, and the church members set up a foster grandparent connection, matching up grandparentless families with grandchildrenless older adults. Often these relationships become very special and enduring. One grandfather told me, "We finally got to California for Thanksgiving and discovered our grandchildren had an older couple coming for dinner—their foster grandparents. At first it made me a little sad and jealous, but I ended up very grateful. We can only afford to visit every two to three years. We became very fond of our substitutes, and there was no rivalry. We decided that when we got back to New Jersey we would suggest this program to our own church and become foster grandparents ourselves."

Some schools and senior citizen groups are now sharing activities. There are camps where older people join in with children; across the generations is an experience that enhances the lives of both young and old. And it need not be a formalized group project. A twenty-three-year-old recovering drug addict told me, "I have a neighbor who is in her eighties. I call her 'Grandma.' I do some shopping for her and she calls me 'my child,' hugs and kisses me, makes me chicken soup when I have a cold, tells me stories about her life as a child in Poland, gives me presents of things that she thought she would save for her grandchildren. But she never married and now she says, well, she didn't have any children, but God gave her a granddaughter. I've been waiting all my life for her." Nurturing children of all ages is our business.

Steady nurturing and reinforcing feelings of self-worth can be hazardous if grandchildren develop a feeling that we are superhuman beings! Some of the advice and information we give when grandchildren are very young seems to them to have come from a Higher Power; they tend to think we always know what we are talking about. A young friend, Jessica, felt that her grandmother was the wisest woman in the world. She seemed to know so many answers; when she said something, it always seemed to turn out the way she said it would. Grandma was

the family "wise woman." Jessica told me, "When I said something really smart to my mother, or when I predicted things
that happened, my mother said, 'You're just like your grandmother.' When I was about twelve and my mother said this, I
suddenly realized Granny had been guessing!" As children get
older, more sophisticated, it is not only parents who develop
clay feet, but grandparents as well. We need to accept this with
good grace as a necessary indication of growing up. It isn't
important that grandchildren perceive us as larger than life. But
even when they may eventually disagree with us and become
far more interested in their own generation, we hope they will
think of us with affection.

Whatever else I may have done with my life, my granddaughter knows that I think she is wise, beautiful, kind, the most
wonderful person in all the world. I hope she has a deep sense
of the connection between the oldest and the youngest generations and the meanings of time and change. Grandparents
help to bind children to the world of human experience, what
it means to be mortal, to live as fully as possible for the time
we are given.

A grandmother told me, "I couldn't figure it out, but my
grandson Danny told me he had to take me to his second-grade
class for show-and-tell. He didn't explain it to my satisfaction,
but he was obviously so insistent that I went with him. The
teacher looked surprised and puzzled when I told her that
Danny had insisted on my coming to school. Suddenly she
laughed and said, 'I bet I know why Danny wanted you to come
to school! Yesterday I told the children to bring "their favorite
thing" to school. I guess you're *it*!' Danny, relieved to have the
explanation made clear, nodded his head solemnly. The teacher
said, 'What a lovely idea! What I'd had in mind were stuffed
animals, favorite toy cars, and dolls.' "

The worthiest goal we can possibly have is to try to be our
grandchildren's favorite thing.

Grandparenting
Resources

American Association of Retired Persons (AARP)
Special Projects—Midge Marvel, Anne Studner
1200 East Carson Street
Lakewood, CA 90712

American Self-Help Clearinghouse
St. Clare's-Riverside Medical Center
Denville, NJ 07834

Foundation for Grandparenting
Dr. Arthur and Mrs. Carol Kornhaber
12 Sheldon Road
Cohasset, MA 02025

Grandparents Against Immorality and Neglect (GAIN)
Betty Parbs
720 Kingstown Place
Shreveport, LA 71108

Grandparents As Parents (GAP)
Sylvie de Toledo
Psychiatric Clinic for Youth
2801 Atlantic Avenue
Long Beach, CA 90801

Grandparents/Children's Rights, Inc.
Lee and Lucile Sumpter
5728 Bayonne Avenue
Haslett, MI 48840

Grandparents in Divided Families
Marjorie Slavin, Edith S. Engel
Scarsdale Family Counseling Service
405 Harwood Building
Scarsdale, NY 10583

Grandparents Raising Grandchildren
Barbara Kirkland
P.O. Box 104
Colleyville, TX 76034

Grandparents Rights Organization (GRO)
Richard S. Victor, Esq.
555 South Woodward Avenue, Suite 500
Birmingham, MI 48009

Second Time Around Parents
Michele Daly
Family and Community Services of Delaware County
100 West Front Street
Media, PA 19063

PUBLICATIONS, NEWSLETTER, AND VIDEOTAPE

Grandparents
Scarsdale Family Counseling Service
405 Harwood Building
Scarsdale, NY 10583

New Horizons
Grandparents Reaching Out
141 Glensummer Road
Holbrook, NY 11741

Vital Connections
Foundation for Grandparenting
12 Sheldon Road
Cohasset, MA 02025

When Mom and Dad Break Up
Hollace Brown
Home Video
Paramount Pictures
5555 Melrose Avenue
Hollywood, CA 90038

Bibliography

GENERAL REFERENCE

Ahrons, C. R., and M. E. Bowman. "Changes in Family Relationships Following Divorce of Adult Child: Grandmother's Perceptions." *Journal of Divorce*, Vol. 5, pp. 49–68.

American Bar Association. *Grandparent Visitation Disputes: A Legal Resource Manual*, ed. Ellen C. Segal and Naomi Karp. Chicago: American Bar Association, 1989.

Bloomfield, Harold H., M.D. *Making Peace with Your Parents*. New York: Ballantine Books, 1985.

Boyd, R. R. "The Valued Grandparent: A Changing Social Role," in W. T. Donahue, J. L. Kornbluh, and B. Power, eds., *Living in the Multigenerational Family*. Ann Arbor, Mich.: Institute of Gerontology, 1969.

Cherlin, A., and F. F. Furstenberg. "Styles and Strategies of Grandparenting," in V. L. Bengtson and J. F. Robertson, eds., *Grandparenthood*. Beverly Hills, Calif.: Sage, 1985.

———. *The New American Grandparent.* New York: Basic Books, 1986.

Elkin, Meyer, M.S.W. "Conciliation Courts: The Reintegration of Disintegrating Families," in *The Family Coordinator*, Conciliation Court of Supreme Court of Los Angeles County (January 1973).

———. "Grandparents Are Also Forever," in *Conciliation Courts Review*, Vol. 15, No. 2 (December 1977).

Foster, Henry H., and Doris Jonas Freed. "The Child's Right to Visit Grandparents," in *Trial* (March 1984).

Francke, Linda Bird. *Growing Up Divorced*. New York: Linden Press/ Simon & Schuster, 1983.

Johnson, C. L. "Grandparenting Options in Divorcing Families: An Anthropological Perspective," in V. L. Bengtson and J. F. Robertson, eds., *Grandparenthood*. Beverly Hills, Calif.: Sage, 1985.

Kornhaber, Arthur, M.D., and Kenneth L. Woodward. *Grandparents/ Grandchildren: The Vital Connection*. Garden City, N.Y.: Anchor Press/Doubleday, 1981.

Laiken, Deidre S. *Daughters of Divorce*. New York: William Morrow, 1981.

Matthews, S. H. "Adolescent Grandchildren's Evaluations of Their Relationships with Their Grandparents." Paper presented at thirty-sixth annual meeting of Gerontological Society of America, San Francisco (November 1983).

New York Law Journal. Second Judicial Dep't., Appellate Div. *Kampf*, res., v. *Worth*, ap. (February 22, 1985).

Nichols, Michael P., Ph.D. *The Power of the Family*. New York: Simon & Schuster, 1988.

Paskowicz, Patricia. *Absentee Mothers*. New York: Universe Books, 1984.

Pellegrin, Daniel S., J.D. "Mediation Services for the Supreme Court: A Proposal to Develop an Alternative Mechanism Outside the Formal Adjudicatory Process to Resolve Marital Dispute Cases." White Plains, N.Y.: Family Mediation Associates, n.d.

Pennsylvania Superior Court. *Miller* v. *Miller* (May 25, 1984).

Rosenthal, C. J., V. W. Marshall, and J. Synge. "The Succession of Lineage Roles as Families Age," in *Essence*, Vol. 4, pp. 179–193.

Wallerstein, J. S., and J. B. Kelly. *Surviving the Breakup: How Children and Parents Cope with Divorce*. New York: Basic Books, 1980.

Wallerstein, Judith S., Ph.D., and Sandra Blakeslee. *Second Chances*. New York: Ticknor & Fields, 1989.

Wilcoxon, S. Allen. "Grandparents and Grandchildren: An Often Neglected Relationship Between Significant Others," in *Journal of Counseling and Development*, Vol. 65 (February 1987).

BOOKS GRANDPARENTS CAN BUY
FOR THEIR GRANDCHILDREN

Blume, Judy. *It's Not the End of the World.* Scarsdale, N.Y.: Bradbury Press, 1972.

Gardner, Richard A. *The Boys and Girls Book About Divorce.* New York: Bantam Books, 1971.

Krementz, Jill. *How It Feels When Parents Divorce.* New York: Alfred A. Knopf, 1984.

LeShan, Eda. *Grandparents: A Special Kind of Love.* New York: Macmillan, 1984.

ABOUT THE AUTHOR

EDA LESHAN, noted author of more than twenty-five books, including *It's Better to Be Over the Hill Than Under It* and *When Your Child Drives You Crazy*, holds a master's degree in child psychology, and has been an educator and family counselor for more than forty-five years. She writes a weekly syndicated column for *Newsday*, and regularly contributes to *Woman's Day*, *Parents*, and other national magazines. She lives in New York City and on Cape Cod, where she is near her daughter, Wendy, and her granddaughter, Rhiannon.

Ask for these titles at your local bookstore, or order from:

Newmarket Press
18 East 48th Street, New York, NY 10017
(212) 832-3575   Fax: (212) 832-3629

Please send me:

LeShan, IT'S BETTER TO BE OVER THE HILL THAN UNDER IT
_____ $11.95 paperback (1-55704-251-9)

LeShan, IT'S BETTER TO BE OVER THE HILL THAN UNDER IT
_____ $18.95 hardcover (1-55704-071-0)

LeShan, I WANT MORE OF EVERYTHING
_____ $11.95 paperback (1-55704-247-0)

LeShan, I WANT MORE OF EVERYTHING
_____ $20.00 hardcover (1-55704-211-X)

LeShan, GRANDPARENTING IN A CHANGING WORLD
_____ $11.95 paperback (1-55704-307-8)

LeShan, GRANDPARENTING IN A CHANGING WORLD
_____ $19.95 hardcover (1-55704-175-X)

_____ Total books ordered

Subtotal: $ _____

* Plus shipping and handling: $ _____

NY residents add Sales Tax: $ _____

TOTAL AMOUNT: $ _____

*For postage and handling add $3.00 for the first book, plus $1.00 for each additional book. Allow 4-6 weeks for delivery. Prices and availability subject to change.

I enclose check or money order payable to NEWMARKET PRESS in the amount of $ _____.

Name _____

Address _____

City/State/Zip _____

For discounts on orders of five or more copies. contact Newmarket Press, Special Sales Department, 18 East 48th Street, New York, NY 10017. (212) 832-3575.

leshpb.8/95